Crank Shaped Notes

ARROWSMITH
PRESS

Crank Shaped Notes
Thomas Sayers Ellis
© 2021 Arrowsmith Press
All Rights Reserved

ISBN: 978-1-7346416-6-0

Second Edition

Boston — New York — San Francisco — Baghdad
San Juan — Kyiv — Istanbul — Santiago, Chile
Beijing — Paris — London — Cairo — Madrid
Milan — Melbourne — Jerusalem — Darfur

11 Chestnut St.
Medford, MA 02155

arrowsmithpress@gmail.com
www.arrowsmithpress.com

The thirty-fifth Arrowsmith book was typeset & designed
by Ezra Fox for Askold Melnyczuk & Alex Johnson
in Baskerville typeface

Cover Design by Aliaja Allison

Crank

THOMAS

Shaped

SAYERS

Notes

ELLIS

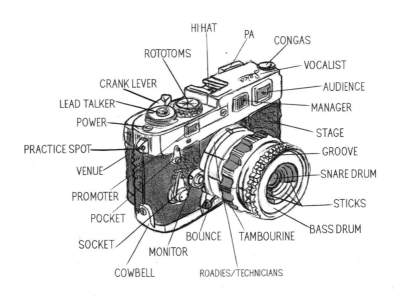

HI·HAT   PA   CONGAS

ROTOTOMS   VOCALIST

CRANK LEVER   AUDIENCE

LEAD TALKER   MANAGER

POWER   STAGE

PRACTICE SPOT   GROOVE

VENUE   SNARE DRUM

PROMOTER   STICKS

POCKET   BASS DRUM

SOCKET   BOUNCE   TAMBOURINE

MONITOR

COWBELL   ROADIES/TECHNICIANS

Acknowledgements

"Chuck Town" originally appeared on KROnline (*Kenyon Review*) with a recording performed by Heroes Are Gang Leaders, Fall 2015.

"The Helicopter" originally appeared in *Words. Beats. Life* and was reprinted in chapbook form by Willow Books in 2011.

"Polo Goes to the Moon" appeared in *The Paris Review*, Number 209, Summer 2014; and on *The Paris Review*'s website with "Amiri's Green Chim Chim-knees Growth Tribe," a recording performed by Heroes Are Gang Leaders, Fall 2014.

The author wishes to thank Tony Bolden, guest editor of "The Funk Issue" of the *American Studies Journal* (Vol. 52, No. 4, 2013); Kevin Coval, Quraysh Ali Lansana and Nate Marshall, co-editors of *The BreakBeat Poets: New American Poetry in the Age of Hip Hop* (Haymarket Books, 2015); Ellen Doré Watson and Pam Glaven, editors of the *Massachusetts Review* (Autumn 2013, Vol. 54, Issue 3) and its Digital Chapbook Series and Askold Melnyczuk, editor of Journal (Volume 12), Arrowsmith Press, where excerpts from this book originally appeared.

A few of these notes were included in the production of "Drums Along the Potomac" and performed by the author with Burnt Sugar (conducted by Greg Tate and featuring Marc Cary, Donnell Floyd (D Floyd), Milton "Go-Go Mickey" Freeman and Kenny "Kwick" Gross at the Lincoln Center (David Rubenstein Atrium) in New York City, May 16, 2013 and at the Kennedy Center for Performing Arts (Millennium Stage) in Washington, D.C., May 20, 2013.

Special Dedications to Zoma Wallace, curator of the exhibition "Go-Go Swing, Washington, D.C.'s Unstoppable Beat" (D.C. Commission on the Arts & Humanities), September 2013, where selections from this book were briefly showcased.

ABM at the GoGo Rally Against Police Brutality, 2007

for Bobbie Westmoreland

Part I

Lat: Capitol 38° 53′ N.
Long. ———— 0° 0′

Bob Cicero of Globe Poster Printing Corp., 2011

I

Money burns the pocket, pocket hurts.

Jean Toomer

Stick Bag Perspective

A pair of slim-lengths, born and raised in the District, the District of Columbia, D.C., not Washington, D.C. Sticks that feel and think and speak (percussively) from being beaten and from being used to beat. Sticks that became a name. Sticks used to write. The Sticks I am. I am the beat, the wooden go-between. Use me. I get used, held, handled and hurled against the sound making of hurt. Use me the way Junk used "Use Me." I won't wither, won't splinter. Skinny, very skinny, bones-in-skin skinny for years; and then made smooth and fast (roll-fast) and sharp, mentally and emotionally, sharp enough to fit in the spaces between chrome rims and curbs, and sharp enough to fit in the avenue-like angles in ideas where the intellect—like the streets and their classroom-confined corners—were often as loud as the sun reflecting off of a pair of marching, twirling cymbals—and not a whispered traffic like the kind created by a journalist or a sip of gossip or a snitch (not mere telling) but the active, healthy thing that comes from motion and gives birth via sound becoming physical then the flesh spreading itself thin enough to become liquid then breath, the atmosphere to what we know as stance, style and exchange, where to "be at," the beat, a heart, where to morph (or to be from), the heat, a head with eyes in it, ideas in it, dreams that survive their own dead ideas.

I wish I could act as just one but I am not one. I am two, held by one who uses two, two belonging to several, unsevered, a many of multiple human kinds, a many a-talking-to, twice spoke, double speak, the speed of one tongue racing another tongue, more than one mouth, more than one mouth, say it again, say it more than once, two sticks, and if you were born and raised in the District then you have probably and possibly either had to use hands or heard hands being used. Stick and move like the one with Sugar at the beginning of his name. A bear will tell you, "the sweetest things knock you out. The bitter ones awake you." A hunter with a trombone too.

Let the misuse slide and learn from it. Taught to pray, to boost, to foreplay. Taught, too, to obey a map that was more corporate than organic. Pre DMV (District, Maryland, Virginia). Note: They say "DMV" to shrink you, to make you think that the area of your current geographic circumference is equal to the one surrounding it—socially, culturally, psychologically and politically. The shrinking creates agenda. The agenda creates service. The service creates revenue. The revenue is an avenue. The avenues encompass you in citizenship. Independence, Constitution, Pennsylvania. To control you, your energy forced to travel the asphalt of state names and diagonal roads.

If only you could see you from above, your rapid spiritual ascensions, your faster than walking movement, that national needle pointing upward out of two interlocking circles. If only you could count the accentuations before they shrink, un-emphasized, in unaffordable air and unaffordable water. All the gates between the scandals. All the scandals between the handlers. All the handlers between the hearings. The price tag that harbors a harbour set in handwriting by the same someone who said, "We ought to auction Anacostia to ourselves." The long con of grabbing land via temporary rentals. It cost the Necostines, the dark Nescostines, their loves and their lives. The Necostines—so named by Captain John Smith, a version of the man who said we had to go at the end of all those early GoGos in the 70s, 80s and 90s.

If you were born and raised, here, in Columbia's District, ask yourself where do I live—near a park, near a monument, on a hill, Jenkins Hill? Ask your other self, remembering that there are two of you, two-in-one, why do I live here—birth, chance, heritage, Residence Act (1790), class?

I am almost certain that you do not have a scenic view of either branch of governance or flow, except for when you are running to catch public transportation, late for work, whose work, theirs or yours? I am not here to glorify the groove just to say that you can learn about what's above you and below you from it.

Being a handheld thing, a thing being used, identical things in the mood for dents and to be dented, I am just like you, "from the sticks" as they say. You are just like me, the great turtle rising out of water, flowing from something and into something. We are not the alchemy that makes the muse sick, that changes the spelling of the spirit of it to music. We share the length of the journey. We share the tip. We share the top. We spin. We click against rims. Toms know we are coming but enjoy the anticipation and expect the contact. The contact is communication. Hidden in the length of the journey, English. The syntax begins near the snare. It sounds like snake, synthesizes like air.

We have no idea why you call what you make us do—strokes, rolls and rudiments. Raised above the rehired air traffic of copper-based bronze circles, we start the supreme how of the show. The shirtless, seated one counts off. Seems there's always some rule of governance, some sequence, in the flow. Beat: be at pattern. Paradiddles to Flam accents to Single Dragadiddles to Double and Triple Ratamacues. On some serious breathing, on some serious Bureau of Language Management (BLM), we formulate the flow no matter what time we arrive. Our daily patterns tell us, percussively, that we are certainly too poor to properly enjoy, privately, the currency of the Potomac River.

In 2019, we became Official, we became re-owned, a muse of our own home. Home Rule became ruled home. The first official use of the name Anacostia was in 1793. Told they need money, "money, money, money," the natives are still paying for the use of the new arrangement of their original name. The pre-Copyright of Wrongness. No royalties because the thieves are always Royalty, the Royals. Like a constantly narrowing repetition of narrative, the perspective overlaps till the prose becomes percussive and lyric. The tribe was called the Natcotchtank. Perhaps it was the imposing of the outsider's religion on the natives that changed "tank" to river.

Junk Yard Junkies and Junkettes, 2010

1

Those who control the board, the Control Board, keep us in conflict and without monitors so that we do not properly hear ourselves or each other, nor are we allowed to decide when to release the shutter of our own communities, when to frame and when to print. It is not its own boss, the Control Board.

2

If your cowbell
has a bent mouth
and a stick-dent

in its identity,
it's probably because
some jealous bammas

thought it
was a contact sheet
of images

and jumped-it,
onstage, between hands & bands,
where you left it.

3

All of the debris from all of the bombs we dropped in the 1980's is still here, under the bridge, where we left it, because it was never safe in our pockets next to the keys "somebody (other than us) lost." Waiting to explode, a flash on the hot shoe of our collective native feet, one that forces the entire city and nation to blink, through the lens, though they will unmake every life in the wave file and say we did it to blow ourselves up, say we did it through the lens, to strike back at them, for predatory listening.

4

Like a y-shaped question,
like a moment of land embracing the absence of self,
the Potomac River is the eldest citizen
   in Washington
and, like a living library,
   only it knows the secret
as to why the power keeps going out:
   The eastern branch
   is hiding free energy!

5

Retro Day-Glo, not Retro-cession

There is no such place as the DMV. We must never forget the results of
the violence of 1847 when 31 of the 100 square miles ceded to the District
were returned to Virginia. Like a shady ode to the VA in Ovation, imagine
the amount of manufactured radiance that would be lost if a large section
of your favorite, classic GoGo Poster were torn off.

Major League Announcement: Crank has no geographic boundaries
and the time has come for D.C. GoGo to stop punishing the Brothers
and Sisters of GoGo Virginia for the placement of rivers and bridges.
Every bridge has two sides, and their missions should be geocentric, not
egocentric. Crank does not revolve about the sound of the sun. The sons
and daughters of sound revolve around crank. Out of many, Mr. Armani.

6

Swole because all you do is eat, drink and sleep the beat but nothing puts
reality to the test like an enlarger so "don't play with Sugar" or any other
legal crank thinners.

7

I put a buck in the bucket and the junk-youngins' kept workin', muthafuckin'
ruff it.

8

I am tired of the hyphen.
It makes
Go-Go stutter.

9

Come "ro," come "to," come "tom." Come "twi," come "twis," come
"twist," come "twisted," come turn a clear ear to the un-tuned pioneers.
Come tune them nearer. Initial your own crank, be your own acronym
revolt because even with one leg up, the young bounce higher (in percussive
protest) than the old but the old are the foundation, the ground, the grid
and grind, without which there wouldn't be any young.

10

Hip Hop may break studio-dawn all night long but GoGo percussions the
concert-sun till the lights come on.

11

A tube full
of rub-on in-womb groove,

                                        body-snatching any bodies
                                        if they don't move their bodies.
That's what
the pocket feels like, a roll of roll-with-it, unprotected non-crank protection.

Our inability to identify the stages and layers of Cultural Revolution have tricked us into a belief that GoGo is nonpolitical and not a Resistance Movement. There are three branches of GoGo (Groove, Crank and Bounce) and when they share "the floor," they move the people in the back, against the wall, up from the bottom of the poor representation that accompanies indifferent listening. Neither manual or D.C. GPS is needed and no lawmaker, paid or possessed, not even the one who signed the Crank Bill of Rights, can navigate the transitory drama between the branches without acknowledging the repossessed empire in party.

13

Elders groove, adults crank, youngins' bounce. All three strands have ways of building and chaining bodies to tides but how do we mend and strengthen the ripped pocket lining between Da Old Heads and Da Young Feet? The bridge represents DNA and, therefore, saying "gimme" is not enough. From the mother tongue, a new day, Adebayo, a new day.

14

Bounce to the suburbs if you want but poor people are the lining in that pocket too, and that is why anti-percussion hides its hands in the hood where it easily reaches in, blending and easing (like counterintelligence) before exiting—whenever they need people to blame and whenever they need escape-votes...they create homes like large boxes (minus the tripod), shifting film plates, empty plates and peace signs after each shot.

15

We have just three words for whoever voted to get rid of...and whoever enforced the disappearance of day and the classic Day-Glo Globe posters, "Sho Yuh Wrong!"

Washington's famous humidity is not a result of the swamp it was built on, the sweltering tensions arise from the "hot chopped bar-b-que" between local and federal interests and from the decisive moments caused by the coming Golgotha in GoGo.

> They eat on a hill.
> We beat
> on a river.

17

Keep your wallets in the pocket, your nickels, dimes and quarters in the socket. Put the pedal to the metal, roto-beats bounce. Check the account of both feet before you deposit. Put a foot in the sock, twist the key in a lock.

18

Short rolls within the groove and long rolls to finish the groove, but the best way to knock a bamma Mayor who ain't in the band and who ain't supposed to be onstage off the stage is with the base of a mic stand. A base is what every local, homegrown candidate needs to protect it from a pre-programmed and synthesized Federal sting. No base metal, bass drum, pedal to the metal, basic matter or free base of metallurgy is free.

19

The transplants are planning to stuff all of the homeless people in D.C. into congas and roll them into the Potomac River. Thirsty plants need to do dirt and are doing this to drown sound not to rid, via housing, the Nation's Capital of its homeless population. However, like the bellies of time capsules, the congas will prove themselves soundproof.

The word rototom looks like a set of rototoms.

dot dot dot

tom tom tom

stand

21

The lead talker is the Speaker of multiple Houses on multiple stages and hills. We, the People, with our hands in the air, are our own Congress. Outside the pocket there are laws one must never break. Inside the pocket you can't survive unless you break laws, break them all the way down. Often mistaken for a picture-making cowbell, cameras, too, are full of percussive programs and breakaway projects like Pratt's.

22

With the help of the police, the local government, and perhaps the Church of the Imaginary Day that binds you to the circle of the week, any groove-addicted recruit can become a useful lead snitch.

23

Speaking of percussive resistance, maybe movement (not violence) killed GoGo's chance of owning its own home (at home) and becoming the real estate of the people. The pocket heard violence say, "I was too busy, dancing" and the socket say it heard dancing say, "I was too busy, fighting."

24

You think you "boogie flat" and "boogie round" but what if the wagon (like a minimum wage) got on you instead of the other way around? Would you still do-the-do on down? Ain't it good to you has to be good to somebody other than just you and if it ain't, then it ain't funky or worthy of the hot, cold, sweat bodies abused by federal air-conditioning.

25

To refer to Chuck Brown as "Pops" suggests a certain familiarity and respect for a shared and kindred intimacy with the GoGo Community. He was not Pops to everyone. There was Chuck Brown, locally and nationally known, and there was "Chuck," for D.C. not Washington. There was also "Mr. Don't Give A Fuck," known as such to the locals who survived nights in the trenches of small clubs with him, the ones who saw him break up fights and threaten to join them.

"Chuck Baby" came later as a replacement for "Bamma Chuck." Chuck was voted and proudly accepted the award for Bamma of the Year in the mid 70s. There was also "The Godfather of GoGo," a symbol of local integrity, pride, and a reminder of the cultural chain of command.

Then there was "Pops," a usage strictly for young insiders, specifically (though not exclusively) the musicians who earned the privilege by playing with him on the D.C. GoGo scene and by living inside his sound and being nurtured by it.

If you got close enough, you heard his daughter and sons call him dad, even closer and you might have heard his wife call him "Baby." I called him Chuck and Mr. Brown although he once said to me at a soundcheck, "Call me Pops, that's what most young gentlemen who I raised call me."

No former Soul Searcher, to my knowledge, ever called him Pops. If you play GoGo or attended public school in one of D.C.'s pre-furnished stations of the compass—NW, NE, SW, SE—you've got Pops in your pocket.

I gave him my camera once and he held what he got till I got what I needed.

Chuck Brown, 2011

Polo Goes to the Moon

Reginald Valentino Burwell, Jr.
1971–2013

There's been
a lot of talk,
lately, as to whether
or not America
actually went
to the moon.
The nonbelievers
say there's no
weather in Space
—no humidity, no wind, no rain,
only empty pockets
and crank shapes.
Craters, big-ass
asteroids, black holes.
They say waving
our arms, all at once,
is as false as the flag
and we say We, We the people,
percussively agree:
Astronaut-Bouncing
jive-like looks phony, unless,
of course, you think of the moon
as a snare drum
—half, eclipsed, full,
and consider, as Polo did,
the percussive
nature of gravity,
the forcible way the Earth,

like a party, pulls
a body, every body
back to it…every time
some symbol crashes
or the rototoms,
like satellites,
get too-hype and someone
jumps up, as Polo did,
beyond the
regular "lock" of
solar system
like a short, well-barbered
meteor, hurled
into the divine orbit
of coma…beyond the limitations
of all things earthly,
including the notion
of nation, and its local,
ingrown extension: going National.
The whole time
Polo was in the air,
he was in total control
of his own ounce
of lunar sleep,
replacing the handcuffs
around Saturn
with open hi-hats.
The whole time
he was on
life support,
alphabetized,
removing vowels.

Cardboard Cutout of Reginald "Polo" Burwell, 2011

LP Skate Boys, 2008

The pocket does not dream of leaving home but when in bed with other cities, home has often left the pocket out of its dreams, why, because if you crank all-night after night after night, it's not crank anymore. It's a drug.

Like Congress, class is in session with Class Band because the gears and gadgets of GoGo, its squirts and spanks, their mighty musculature, culture and tradition, can teach, can school, the Federal Government how to properly balance every empty pocket in the tide of horn, those brown bones, and the tidy of talk. If you want us to pull our pants up, add more economic exits to the Beltway not more Aggression.

> Even azz it claps,
> resistance is its
> own clenched
> House vote.

Dear Person-in-the-Pocket photographer, if your lens is longer than a cowbell, please, either leave it in your car or close your eyes when shooting. Intimacy is as percussive as percussion is intimate. GoGo Photography is physical. Get close. Be bumped. Bump back. Snap. Let the camera be the hand on the hip of the person you did not know you were dancing with, functionary-close. Let the focal length ride!

GoGo keeps stating and restating the holding pens of its local Statehood (NW, NE, SW, SE) because GoGo wants the high and low call of hood status, but unknown to GoGo, Washington, D.C. is a city-state, a station of the seat of empire, a privately owned corporation, one of three tiers.

So, what if you can't read their music in their way; they can't play your pocket in your way. Everyone is illiterate, at first, when they are away from home but literate, always, inside of themselves. One of the things that money wishes it were is water. The other is music.

> Music comes
> from within the water
> within
> non money.
> Money is man's one eye.

You are not a script-driven actor on a staff of notes imprisoned in time signature. The industry within you contains many idioms, organic orchestras and chambers of celestial festivals, many Da Grew'ps. And either you believe in the civilizations within you or you don't, but if you don't then get out of the way of the inner conductor because you will never go anywhere in human matter that matters.

31

I'd rather be an old, single, beaten cowbell addicted to the hardest drink at the bar than an entire, well-dressed setlist-dependent Grown and Sexy Band. There's nothing worse than Pharmaceutical Groove. Get those cheat sheets off the stage so the lead talker can voice more than two sheets to the wind and fight like an anthem because this condition is critical.

32

Photographing Chuck Brown's hands, I was reminded of the loosely clasped, bright moment on the cover of *Bustin' Loose*. *The Lord of the Rings* also worried my mind. Three rings on the cover, the king's jewels for a glove. Seven rings around Saturn. Surrounded by blue, Saturn is the record label's logo. Most of the sound from that light, the search for a source or a turn away from our former sun, has yet to reach us.

33

You know the pocket
is all about parenting
with a purpose,

            yet another
instructional family discussion
  of reproduction.

  That is why

           you never see
the big congas without their juniors,
those new shiny seeds,
  the ones got from
    having skins hit
     by the birth
of sounds
  in the pelvis of hands.
   Gon bops.

34

You can't have crank-shaped logic without a crank-shaped appetite. Crank must fast. Crank must feast. The 1 mic is the mind of crank. The 2 mic is the mouth of crank. The bass drum is the rebirth center of all tribal three-course meals. In the throat of crank, the stones of the city grow from the soft, dented walls like chewable marble. Do not refrigerate crank. Low crank-esteem destroys the meaty barracks of character.

35

A percussive way of sense is not a rhythmic way of sense but a rhythmic way of sense can be a vocal way of sense if and when the uptown yard out back cries the siren of full vocal-feeling, Weansey, feeling vocal.

Maurice "Moe" Shorter, 2008

36

If it wasn't for the level of plastic bucket in their stomachs, the empty tins of sardines in their cupboards, we might not have the socket. When the meals got short, shorter by the moment, the junk got good and cranked through hunger.

37

Like subject-verb agreement the physical grammar of a GoGo frontline used to be linear, used to be a line of ears, a uniformed unit, but that was before "The Show" and "La Di Da Di" and before Footz opened the hi-hat like a pair of sharp, brass scissors; that's when natural speech, pure non-rhymed lead talk (in the pocket) began its first phase of decline. That's when Go Hip and Hop Go and Pocket Rap began. That's when natural, input-output, two-way listening thinned.

38

Cover a thing so you can't see it. Cover a thing so you can't hear it. Who programs and formats your senses? Who codes the camera so that you think, while shooting, that you are in control of the choices, all made by chance and Chance, a second-tier band. The thing you want most is Free Will but the meddler in the middle of the medium, radio, is pushing Free Won't.

39

No homegrown shadow ever ran off and became a Senator. No local pastor ever mentioned how, in Greek, "holy ghost" means breathing. No tidythetalker or city council member ever admitted that the city, not the community, are the consumers of human life. And no council of noblemen ever allowed its ranks to be infiltrated, by any level of monitor man, without a full social and percussive vetting, even the backup sidepiece is investigated by one of the manager's reliable henchmen, by Bacchus.

By the time I perceive the picture through the viewfinder, I've missed the photographic moment and by the time you grab your Crew (hold up a peace sign or middle finger) and pose, what was left of the photographic moment has weakened even more—like a visual version of slumming. Distance plus pose time equals the rhythm of composition. The picture, or flick as you call it, sounds bad. A photograph that sounds good should meet or beat your feet to the full possibility of the frame. A peace sign is sign language. There is nothing less percussive than a silent photograph.

41

Pure crank counters privilege. In fact, its socio-percussive-political value reunions a frontline akin to a rare and highly contagious form of prolific-triflin' but don't get it twisted till it's un-tuned, the pocket is not impoverished. All of dem hands, info feet and vocal newsfeed, damage by Gamage, make its reach: a beat to teach and impover-rich!

42

God bless community Recreation Centers (also known as Recs) for giving our noises a place to become grooves and our grooves a place to become songs, unknown and ignored, often near a playground. In the lyric tradition of natural wetness and wellness, our sweat flowed, in those physical exercise centers.

43

I miss the days when the Hammond B3 was used to foreshadow a groove, the easing before entering, like an organic literary device. The pocket used to contain so much foresight and foreplay, and the grooves were intimately structured—touch, taste, talk, togetherness. Your organ did not orgasm without a Leslie. Without keys your fingers did not please. Without warms chords, you were a three-minute lover surrounded by clouds of cold joy.

44

The loudest part of GoGo may be the beat, the hard relationships of its elements, but the loudest part of the beat is still poverty—the dependence on banknotes. Like it or not, those are poor hands in your pocket. Get in. Get out. Every time some promoter tries to make their loud, payola world round, percussive pattern-makers re-flatten it. A true map of the "wholetime," the thing you can't buy, is what poor folks need, not money.

45

By the end of the show all four skins should be hot enough to burn the hands off of any bamma (who even thinks about employing them), excluding the cool palms of the conga player. He be-working them joints, every time, like it's the last day of the week and tomorrow is the first imbursement of a new, divine payday.

46

for Greg "Googie" Burton

The straightest alignment in GoGo is the one between the sound source and the stage. It operates like a ley line connecting the prominent structures within the pocket to the crowd. A keyless entry, ordained in blood, a ley line is the amplified light that makes all modes of crank a sacred site, a kingdom.

47

The Black Hole (formerly known as Celebrity Hall), which includes knowledge of the entire biblical / anatomical behavior of the cosmos, alteration of the original lunar sky clock, the extrusion of the sun and the moon, our division into sexes, and the akashic record of our Atlantean and Lemurian Ancestors, was all full of violence, precise cycles of pleasure, fire mist, human mineral and spheres higher than egos long before the inheritance of priceless heritage.

48

With or without security clearance, with or without flow, let it flow, let the floor become one of importance and improvisation not redundancy and permanence, neither routine or asphalt road, but a river, a growth, a groove in the earth, crank not crater-shaped.

49

To stand in the crowd, camouflaged in cameras, like a human shutter at a shooting. To unexpectedly lift the lid of every eye within the reach of the sight that fights light. To give the lead talker, without peering through the viewfinder, the earn your drummer look.

50

I like to wind the camera from behind the drummer where the crank sits.

Adia Danyell Doores, 2007

GoGo Orlando, 2010

The Helicopter

Benny Anthony Harley
1963–2010

Born busy
and still busy,
the hit and run hovering,
a silhouette
in the moon's
spotlight.

One, two, three shows a night,
fingers pressing and releasing the rooftops of valves.
Take off and land vertically,
hover, fly forwards, backwards and laterally.
Like a red and white air ambulance,
trumpet—a propeller, spinning. Southeast,
next Northwest, weekday gigs split in the private rooms
where rotors are kept, Panorama and Maverick.
Once he landed, leg in a cast, outside
the historic Howard Theater, lunchin' hard.
All passengers transported safely,
Carter Barron to Club LeBaron,
homecoming to stadium, Inter-High proms.

A Rare, Master,
Legend, Utensil,
Young Dynamo
of the Golden Age,
baby Soul Searcher,
the Soul Man
  of GoGo.

Tambourines, the round wooden ones,
didn't even have anatomy
before the spiral patterns of Benny's signature,
the way he would shake it with one hand,
stick the other hand through it
like a magician, then strike it with the other hand,
twist of wrist, hard palm, forearm flick.
Little Mafioso hype-man, in a vest, next to Chuck,
sometimes he wore it around his arm like an engagement
elbow ring or bracelet, married to GoGo.
His voice could syce the wind.

> "Said we gonna take some time
> just to watch what you doin'.
> We need that spotlight
> so we can see what you doin'.
> Let's get that spotlight together,
> so we can take some time out
> to watch y'all boogie down now!"

All of D.C. used to *stay open* like a block party in summer.
The bridge he blew, but a groove he built,
        vamped in organ warmth,
friendship, the granddad of Godfava trust.
Traffic signs, a siren, blinking traffic lights.
Miss Mack, that big white truck, red and white sweats.
An orange show poster on the side
of a mid-range cabinet, the trickiest guy in town.
If James Funk was the noun in their fluid,
grammatical front line, then Benny was the verb,
"Ain't it good to you, yeaaaaaaah boy!"

Wrestler upper
body strength,
shoulders rocking,
but the power still went out.
A step a step a slide,
one mouth, two trumpets,
fall and scream. Left arm, a marching band
bent at the waist, action
added to it, the crank
of showmanship,
Ballou to UDC.

What's more mournful: an empty trumpet stand,
        the closed faces
of old venues, or basements
with Alzheimer's like the one on Xenia?
Memory is a synthesizer, sensitive
as the H in Harley, hurts. All I want is for
that laugh to slip between that top, gap-tooth smile,
in need of monitors, a million more times,
then for every name he ever called to jump back up
on the Roll Call and "Say What,"
"Where you wanna go, Where you wanna go,"
but, in the pocket, death is just a technical difficulty,
a reunion of legends, common as bammas fighting with chairs.
For now, fuss-hushed, a bell chord weeps
and this body moves, no more.

        Finger hook to flare,
        leadpipe to pitch,
        valves, *party-baby-do-it*.

The tuning of slide,
of pistons in casings.
Bootleggers press down.
Promoters half-step.
Dry, tired mouthpieces
breaking into hips.

Who comes to boogie comes to sunrise,
who comes to sunrise comes to rest, who comes to rest
comes to sunset—light's braided remembrance,
the gold wings of sleep, protective casket
colder than anvil case silver. Just like a Libra
—to join the loose blood pressure of white tees,
XL and XXL, the property of our at-risk,
         overweight memories.
It's so hard to bury an Air Sign—the worn clichés
for grief like 'Gone but not Forgotten'
and 'Rest in Peace' never properly shrink to fit.
Let the bad rep end. There is nothing violent
about crashing in one's sleep, but

         "The man said we got to go."
         "When you leave,
         would you please leave carefully."
         "Take him away,
         take him away, take him away."
         "Good night, good morning."
         "Bye bye baby,
         babybabybaby
            byebye."

Anthony "Little Benny" Harley, 2007

Gallery Place Bucket Drummer, 2008

51

Nature does not point to a god of love, neither does percussive photosynthesis, so if there was ever a snitch in the pocket, a definer of good and evil, it was the whistle that replaced the cowbell, the mouth imbued with the breath of man, a little ball in a whirl of respiration following the course of nature.

52

All of the things you play and say—cover songs, hooks, dedications, roll calls, displays, dope jams and chants—should be in the service of liberation and of freeing yourself from the dogma of easily recognizable genre crank. Genre Crank lacks signature and is something of a one size fits all hive march through the pocket. The pocket be in its feelings and its feelings be in the socket so it's hard to find crank wrapped in a multiplicity of native needs, including pleasure which is sometimes a sure plea for percussive sensitivity.

53

Dig the trap, the trap of learning, of "stay in school" but there is nothing or no one in the GoGo Community, simultaneously, more old school and more new school than the drum. It attends every important class because its instructor, the human heart, is all-schools.

54

Let's not romanticize those years when we lost so much. Those years when the managers of GoGo were paranoid of theft. No Ins and Outs. No Cameras. No Recording Devices. No Refunds. Those years we didn't listen, the years we were all bootleggers (one way or another) and followed our orders and bought our recorders. Those years could have been better eyes and ears.

for Godfava, Darrien, Scotty and Marky

Keyboard Double Duos

no longer
sit together
in an L shape.
Like mic stands they stand.
Like ivory twinklers
stuck in seats,

they remind me
of the people
waiting for public transportation
    at bus stops,
and of drivers pretending to be passengers
 comfortable in
a moving shelter.

Damn backdoor openers,
former
transfer hustlers,
who call out all 88 stops,
mid-Occupation, transit-trained.
A full bag of tokens.
Mouth ripped
for speaking out,
fare along the strip
    in a flash
not really chord worthy.

Both hands on the traffic-circle
of the wheel:
Logan, Dupont, Randle
like a mobile Rhodes
whose windows
offer Smart Pass users
a chance to interact
with the sharp flat symbols
  of city planning.

Running for a ride,
we used to respect the creased shirts
of keyboardists,
a patch on the arm
for years of safety and service,
granddad glowing like
    a very old,
wooden memorial
dominating our memories
with a hint of salvation,
bullying all
of Naylor Road,
searching for keys
in the pores in the potholes of pockets,
nothing found above
the arched
                piano doors
            but a keystone,
        entrance guarded by elders,
        their grace-thick gospel
and creek of rocks.

56

A closed hi-hat in a diamond. No airplay and always being treated like less than a tourist in your own home, weighed down, not by the weight of things placed in graves but by graves weighing down the way to things, the way to the mystic center bordered by boundary stones.

57

De'Unique's Eunuch Horn is Code for Kingdom.

The shape of crank, full of percussive poetry and percussive people, a fertile light, contains the tension of life, tight and tightened up, one pocket or pillar for pleasure, the other for pain, two pills, tightened tighter and tightly horn-blown above the dawn of man in the realm between time backed up, safely, all the unique unicorns in the atmosphere.

58

If you look at the stage, sideways, slowly, before the show in that moment after the roadies are done and before the band comes on, you will see the whole alphabet, every consonant and vowel, setting itself to "upset the set-up" in an ancient, architectural, reflective chrome, the one sentence of history, a blend of horizontal timelines, the planned illusion of ruins made new, a phonetics of mics like Corinthian columns in an arboretum.

59

The "flashy stuff" (like extra arm movements and spinning in circles, etc. while playing the congas) is just like the camera flash and truly only necessary when there is not enough available light or enough talent or when the lens is too slow to handle the amount of darkness onstage. Many of the qualities we attribute to skill are, perhaps, really just expressions of physical style. The real purpose of flash and flashiness, for some, may not be to illuminate but to exaggerate.

60

There are a lot of ways of participating in community, a lot of ways of being a body that is a unit of unity. No one body is the whole body of crank. Being in the body of a band, not everyone can be the drummer and not everyone can be the camera. Someone has to be the Fat Man at Breezes who gets in free before 10pm. Someone has to be the Fat Lady who opens her mouth, half court, singing in the win. The m's in community have always been arched mic stands.

61

Pocket Lining

A neck
so sensitive
it demands wetness,
electric lick
and choke.
Good itch-scratching,
chucking, back and forth,
like a flow,
like a cloth
only Crank
can stroke.

62

Born in 1935 and known for his love of hats, Chuck Brown, the Godfather of GoGo, was rarely seen in public without one but did you know that Porky Pig made his Looney Tunes debut in 1935 in a featurette titled, I Haven't Got A Hat which includes a Music Recital and a clanging cowbell. Porky also used to burst (bust loose) through a bass drum at the end of cartoons with his trademark, "Th-Th-Th-That's all folks!" And years later Chuck Brown turned one of Porky's famous stutters into his own brand of a brand new groove.

A beat is just a beat but a beat followed by a beat and followed by another beat with a beat in between the beat and a beat under the beat and a beat on top of the beat and a beat beside the beat is a beating, a continuous one, so regarding so-called battles and beefs between bands and band members, know this: percussion without drama is like GoGo without percussion, gen-tri-fried, and every GoGo percussionists (born and raised in the District) has two very non-Shakespearian pockets of behavior to choose from (1) If you beat your kids now, they will beat their kids later and you will have badass grandkids and (2) If you don't beat your kids now, they will beat you later and you will still have badass grand kids who also beat you. In other words: as does hitting, the beat goes on. We are crank-shaped. We get things twisted, including ourselves, bent...bent... bent from a mysterious form of voter-inequality, imbalance and isolation. When our votes leave us, we have no idea where they go. The same thing that makes a photograph, entrance and exit, makes a pocket, all the dramatic ballots, the polls, the levers, the list of those we lost, a roll call of folks trapped like marble in light.

64

for Michael Neal

Neck Brace

If you got nowhere to remove it, down is where you do it, on down.

> A basin of bass,
> time flushed
> into
>> tide,
> position marked
>> into
> tidal,

a stone of hope,
the crusade from tuning fork
to output jack
to bronze freedom
where bright trees kneel
between the head
and shoulders
of channel and river
and below the northern lobe's
inlet gate
around the apple,
the throat of speech evening ate
just to shorten
its name and knobs
to fingerboard fracture
like a soft reservoir
  of bottom
full of pumped water
and faucet bottom.
Brown granite
and life radiates
from Ned's
  head.

65

Grooving is Getting Along with Folks

but "cranking" is cussin' somebody out. All curse words are percussive and all percussive instruments like to be hit from the front and the back, repeatedly, until the entire club, the booty-built bulk of its grammatical core, screams, "back it on up" and "do it again!"

Today is the day I stop using the camera to see the way I already see and the day I start using the camera to see the way I hear crank. Crank that enters the eye, first, is not the same as Crank that enters the ear. Onstage, senses are exits. Offstage, entrances. That's why you should never breathe in Crank, the bruised air in a drum, traps sensory traffic.

Most of the sound-servants in the band are not playing GoGo. They are playing another genre of music on top of GoGo perhaps one of the genres that preceded GoGo, but they—quite naturally—know how to leave a place for GoGo and when to interrupt their parent genres. It is not enough to have learned how to play a guitar like a guitar, a horn like a horn or a keyboard like a keyboard. The guitar must become a cowbell. A horn a tambourine. The keyboards the congas. Crank is creative unlearning, a disruption, a cleansing and conversion.

Every time
local black familiarity,
the Folk Crew,

takes home for granted,
the Refined Crew,
local black privilege,
picks apart
the unity within

the community's desperate pocket.
That's how crucial
dat Buck is.
Wild.

Crowd listening to Mature Clientele Band, 2009

Any body of knowledge or anybody with knowledge
of Classic Crank
can pose a problem
in the form of a philosophy.
All it takes is a pocket of Plato and a socket of Socrates,
the Bam & Wedge of Childs Play,
or an evening at the Carter Barron,
our first taste of Greek amphitheater
 GoGo.

70

"This Beltway that's around D.C. is almost like a wall here."
Dave Rubin

It may not be a percussive fact (yet) but rumor has it that the Beltway
was designed for use by the U.S. Military in the event of a rebellion by
the (at the time) majority Black population of Washington, D.C. It's like
they built a big speed-limit, 64-mile tambourine noose around our bodies,
communities and parties then punished us for hitting it at any places
other than the allowed exits—not a percussive fact yet but this is what the
composing stick, typeset in crank thought, has begun to transfer to galley.

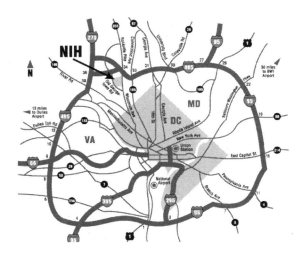

71

There are eight stops on the Metrorail System map that resemble the tops of rototoms. They are the way to freedom. The other seventy-eight stops are visual fake-me outs, non-portals, potholes in the pavement begging for drum keys to twist and tune them so they might reset you to flesh and sentence you to the earthly mindset of overlooking the beauty of local.

72

September 17, 1994

Let us remember the exact location of the geographic-anatomy of loss, the shoulder of Route 50, near Corporate Drive, in Landover, Maryland. There should be a white bowling ball there, the color of his drums, like a blood cell with a pair of sticks coming out of the holes.

73

All that shaking, all that hitting and yet you've probably never properly undressed a tambourine beyond the easy to remove jewelry. In the hands of a man, is a cowbell a woman? In the hands of a woman, is a cowbell a man? The brief lace of rudiments. Only the stick knows which patterns are masculine, which are feminine. Almost a kick. The pocket contains the group chat of gender, chromosomes and song, the anatomy of reproductive toms. There are more open high-hats than there are open closets in GoGo. The full awareness of crank-shaped sexuality can be attributed to nasty and naked drumming. He who peddles the organ. She who tunes the garment.

74

If no one had imitated the Soul Searchers, what would you be doing today, would your personal mythology be a brand? With nothing to say, I would probably be the quietest vowel on Alley Cat's MODX or one of Laura's fingered collective measures in the House of Medici.

All that has
happened within
  our city, socially
and politically,
repeats the beat of itself
  in the pocket,
in patterns,
plaguing the pleasure
  of GoGo.
The looks may change
but the faces,
  the ones you don't
know you know,
are familiar. First a mob then a team
  then a squad
but still a family
only retired
  around the edges
where the percussive life
of service and most
  inner-city hate hides itself,
revealing, again,
that evil has no home-trained
    District Body
      or Building,
that evil is its own live show,
incubated in the silence,
  of savior-inquiry,
nightly, near the PA
nearest prayer.

Nathaniel McKinley Lyles (1963–2012), 2010

Stick Bag Perspective

Years ago, the poetry had already begun, the way poetry begins in the body (not separated from the mind) in sound and sense—feeling for a shape—for what one does not know or has never felt before, all the unknown knotted knowledge that connect and disconnect, repair and sever, the layers of self that exist in flesh.

When it poured, when the poetry would not stop coming, poems were thrown away and the sound they made, their nuance and form, crumbled on the paper planets that imprisoned them as they were catalogued into categories. Before tossing them, I often drew on their blank backs just to peel the percussive façade off of nonreality. The first art I loved was drawing. For all of the rim shots in Dante's drum-kit, a terza rima, the best made stanzas could only hold a portion of the rhythm in any portrait, unlike the toms which could twist and tune and tone to an exact likeness— like, dislike, like, dislike, a preference made less paternal by the intervals in the motion of sticks and the numerous profiles in the patterns, the use of both hands, always looking. Back and forth between the things that taught you to roll, hard and soft, the way you did when your father left.

Well, at least, he came back and made sure you went to more concerts than funerals and before leaving, talked you into the discipline and forms, katas and sparring of Tae Kwon Do (Korean style Karate) that was a necessary preface to your coming fascination with the rudiments of words and drumming, where you became an active student of diagramming grooves, pre-poem poetry, percussive prosody, the process that prepared— not just your ears, but your reverse pouring pores, those holes of sensitive curiosity, to the avalanche of Black voices (African American and the eyes of Otherness) you'd encounter up-in-the Northern South where books with inner beats, full of struggle and pleasure, rushed toward you...for the borrowing, for the buying, for the taking, yes, for the taking and for, eventually, carrying around inside of you until you became one of them or too many of them, walking words.

Call it sacrifice, so-called maturity, either way, you lost many things finding that so-called tree (which confused itself in the service of career), so many things—at times—you didn't even recognize yourself or the selves around you, but you had to look deeply and it hurt...like being born away from your birth without having grown but able to see growth, hear the ground from which growth dies, no soft tissue or paper to transform the wiry ideas of silence into a system of sound, a sound system, one without language or a percussive portal of the substance of life to call parent, not even a blurred version of it, in the stance of what can only be described as the lie of distance.

Scribes describe to de-scribe their own blurry scribble.

They unsubscribe to self. You lost the constant sight of your mother, the feeling-eyes between you, the shared shape of the world, the flat-sphere of vision. It was difficult: watching and not being watched from places like Montgomery, Boston, Cambridge, Providence and Cleveland. The bridge of sound became a hyphen, a pen, keystone and keyboard. Used incorrectly, the hyphen dashed into hours like stabs, not constructive linear steps, toward home, Karl Shapiro's "violent obelisk" that you could never doubt. The best book inside you, your mother.

You were her. She, you.

Fell into mother not from as with the journey from father.

Not a metaphor, a floor. A way and away. Northeast Corridor, a crinkled sentence. A railway of stations. Tickets. Stops. Stats. Names like precise geographic facts. From the Shrimp Boat in D.C. to Beacon Hill in Boston, all aboard. Your father found, not breathing, dead for days, escorted by a spinning record. You wrote a poem about it, cried in the process. Was that the last time another face forced your face to lose wetness? April is like that, literally, a land made of waste. We make the surface of the earth. But before that, when you were unprotected, when your mother worked two jobs and couldn't really keep either one of her eyes on you because of the need for food, because of the need for shelter—where one must live when one is already alive. Apartment. Not a single garden. An evening. after school. I remember my mother was asleep on the couch when it happened, and I knew enough of what I was doing to help it happen although she was older. A child, a surprise, was the child lost to the differences between young accidental parents or did you lose the child, a son, on purpose pursuing school, pursuing words? Can I answer myself (as I have never been able to fashion a response that I was wholly sure of) by quoting a poet, Muriel Rukeyser, "erect in accusation sprung against/a barren sky taut over Anacostia..." Told his name, shown his eyebrows, glimpsed his future in a room full of family one night after a High School newspaper cut and paste session. "Looks just like him," my brother said. Choice on top of choice, fear. Fear on top of fear, choice. "We don't want to lose you to the streets," my High School Counselor said during a random trip to my apartment to find out why I hadn't been to school in a month.

Thank you, Florence Ridley.

Loss was everywhere and the everywhere was no different than in literature. In fact, in writing, people were turning it (loss) into an art—left and right. Sign me up, in public and private, for loss, for losing, for trauma and academic group hurt with a pound of race thrown in all in the name of learning, unlearning and ultimately losing loss, so I could evict (not master) the long-term effects of it.

You lost your rototoms and timbales to college, to knowledge, to not having a ledge, to the Collective so now your instrument is the top seed from which all knowing grows downward into the body toward the feet of crank, shaped by the sound of living and dying close to the ground, not by silence, not by editing, not by the gradual accumulation of degrees.

Thank you, Cool Lou, for the stolen camera.

Up on a speaker, arms swinging, knees being knees in need of bend like a river or things that grow in rings: trees, a snail's shell and ram's horn, you never have to be stuck in just one home, one book or one band ever again. C'mon horns. Let's double it up y'all and use art-sense to play for everyone, and every limb you are, to dodge, to dodge the life sentence of dogmatic singularity.

Big Tony Fisher, 2009

The Anatomy of Syke Dyke

Robert Michael Reed
1958–2008

More tilt in the blood than ill synths,
more space invaders
and pinball in the pocket
than any arcade,

no one did more
with a neck
and the keys of the spine
    than Dyke.

He healed the open bruises
in our hurt-hearing
with the organ.
He made the synthesizer

homeopathic
and a fingered-thing
akin to the percussive acupuncture
of strategic medicine

 like a Sci-fi Sound Artist
of Akashic Record Technology
 reconnecting heads
    to bodies,

Sporty Shorty,
mighty Bison riding
away from the physical world drama
of Cape Nape,

the collared cervix
and source of Strait Crank,
a pure elegance
and a purer allegiance,

only da realist panhandle
   between
the crab in the sky
and pancreatic betrayal
   ordered by

   The Order
   of Day Tone
   Trombone

   like a metal chord of Aprils,
   lead, silver and gold,
an electric rhythm isthmus,
   tours on either side
      of the sea,

stored in the storage unit of still alive,
2 live for life,
too live for live shows,
2 much equipment onstage,

the 50 year-old stem of him,
a bye gone zygote
and a human beanstalk
getting smaller and smaller

like a thing "hey"
might start off right
despite being as wrong
as asking an audience to chant
"Hell Yeah,"

Bomb Squad horns,
constant incoming that should be dancing
misdiagnosed as Not for Sale
promotional copies,

like the tumor
that never tires
of its own rumors,
magnetic resonance imaging,
a moody MOOG.

The problem with Trouble
is that they were giants
and we were Jacks.
Fee-fi-fo-fum.

Larry "Stompdogg" Atwater, 2007

76

I'd rather be a legless booty at a Bounce Beat Rodeo than a bootleg legend locked in a legal battle with my own legs in a crank shaped elegy.

77

Speaking of "keeping it gangsta," according to the Heights Building Act of 1910, which limited the heights of buildings in Washington, D.C. to 110 feet, Big G, Iceberg Slim and Too Tall Steve (Coleman), due to the enormity of their personalities and influence, are illegal, visible miracles that must be protected against homegrown attacks at all times.

78

A GoGo is a form of gathering and being a form of gathering, it is also a form of community organizing even if it is only held together by the ritual of dancing, body law, and the in-the-pocket pride of crank provocateurs coming of age in a city whose identity is a double lie, Nation's Capital and Chocolate City. The moment you add community news (lead listening and lead talking) to the gathering, an exchange between the gatherers and the gathered and more than one talk-cussin' drum (a paroled pocket), the gathering becomes something with purpose, a political possibility, gateless.

79

Regarding artificial light and artificially going live, both being the equivalent of lies in the natural world (if the natural world is natural), every time I raised my camera to the level of chamber to photograph or grab a photograph of a live performance, the cheap paint job of the predictable pattern of my practice attempted to cover the result in mascara, the same way Crew and hood-catering was popular in the 90s; and the same way the blueprint for live performance was turned into sing the hook, rap, sing the hook, rap, sing the hook, breakdown.

80

A little lead talk, like salt, is good for you—especially your boogie body. It can make you sweat. The calcium in the pocket comes from milking the cow and banging the bell. It's an impressive toll, when all the bells resonate the great revelation.

The iron in the pocket comes from putting the foot pedal to the metal. There's nothing healthier or more chewable or more one-a-day than the minutes in a vitamin, how soothing to hear your name roll-called and tossed back at you, amplified, from one respiratory system to another.

When we don't drink enough structured water, the lavish morning ceilings of coffee & crank, the walls we used to work, work us like suckers to death.

81

Can a sound convince you that home is so great that you never want to leave? Were you given a sound to keep you home, home for life, can sound do that, wrap itself around a city (via the people) from the inside out? Everyone one wants to visit the advertised dead things surrounding you but not you, alive you, in your truest home so stop kissing ass and trying to prove that you are equal. Equality cannot be pocketed or proven. Laws are lips.

82

There are a few people who are always in the know in GoGo (call them Engineers) and so many people who always know nothing. The scene really belongs to the latter, the majority know-nothings, but the in-the-knows are faster ambulance chasers than the know-nothings. The know-nothings built GoGo and live GoGo and truly need GoGo but like most workers, they are often tired and sleep from late night shows when the in-the-knows are wide awake, taking over, and twisting all there is to know. The In-the-knows hide the big picture and never take credit for the lack-of-power-state of GoGo.

Anwan "Big G" / Genghis Glover, 2007

83

Walk the streets of D.C., your home, the same way you perform—like everyone in the audience knows you and you have a birth-dirt connection to everyone and everything in the city: past, present and future. And like the very act of beat-breathing, crank life, feet-beating, is the show you can't wait to get to, a show full of continuance, an atmospheric walker, the walker redds of your own reality, going in, go-going, going.

84

It makes sense that a full pocket would party and an empty pocket would punch. The tension makes sense, but the ideal foot-fist must bravely march the wrong punch right out of town, as well as punch the wrong march right out of town. A lot of percussion begins in confusion and a lot of confusion ends in percussion.

85

Our home is unique because it is the seat, the seat of government. The term "Government" is just a political, man-made name for drumming. It should be called Drummer-ment. The drum lets the drummer sit in the seat but the drum, not the drummer, is responsible for its own proper council in the streets, a coalition. A good coalition is like a good PA System seamstress, making sure every pocket has at least three pairs of hands, talking, in it. The drummer is elected by an Electoral Calling not an Electoral College. What is the real meaning of "seat?" Well, if you ever get a chance, practice decoding the underside of the drummer's cymbals, the spirals.

86

Those of us who can remember when there was a black pyramid at each side of the stage—a bass cabinet, a mid-range speaker and a horn—to this very day, we dance and talk jive-slow.

I have a feeling that if Bounce Beat declares itself separate from GoGo, Bounce, being more industrial, will eventually outperform GoGo. I have a related feeling that if Southeast declares itself separate from Washington, Southeast, being more agricultural, will eventually outperform Washington. Maybe Bounce is GoGo and what we thought was GoGo is something else, a replica of R&B and Funk, slowly taking shape. Maybe Southeast is Washington and what we thought was Washington was something else, a replica of Paris and Rome, slowly taking shape, a unification. Perhaps GoGo is only as original as its maverick landowner, Washington, D.C. There is even photographic proof that the landowner is more violent (in the world) than the tenant.

88

Rotunda-to-dome, Rototom-to-drum

GoGo must allow more art into it and the art allowed into it cannot be imitative of anything external nor can it be controlled by it, either. It must be aesthetically pleasing, not just polyrhythmic, but relentless, a poly idea-non mimicry mic check. It must get on its own insular nerves.

89

The sky is clear tonight but I don't see you, not even your faint, local light—out on the town, the real town, eating in healthy restaurants, rolling up and down the avenues, signing autographs and enjoying your status, as a star, on the ground-sky. What kind of eclipse of Disclosure, what kind of City Council black hole is preventing you from standing out in your own nebula, how will you continue as a groove in a galaxy that has a hard time accepting and dealing with non-redemptive, dark matter? It will take you light years to become even a Crew not to mention a cluster in the Constellation of the Sacred, Great Gold Tooth. How will you show, how will you shine if you can't go-hard?

90

The poetry of GoGo has nothing to do with words. The poetry of GoGo occurs in the spaces of parole between locked lives, in the sounds that hold rows of houses together. In fact, the poetry of GoGo is limited by the packaging nature of words, especially words that have never had their plastic heads busted. The poetry of GoGo can hurt any poem that dares to steal its home: up in the air, ready for hands, in the spaces caused by all the banging and by all of the weaponry.

91

The first time you experienced the gears of crank, you felt attacked by it. The second time you did not understand anything it was saying. The third time it broke-off a piece of itself and touched you.with it. The fourth time you were still throbbing (from the third time) in your own new definition of yourself in a new home. The fifth time you grabbed it and begged it not to leave, to stay and protect you but it was too late.

92

When I need to fit more crank than I have room for into a small frame of photography, I simply guess at the distance between me and the crowd, manually focus for that distance, hold the camera either at my chest or over my head slanted downward, close my eyes, then push the button.

93

You think this thing called GoGo cannot save you. You think it is just another noise and unimportant but what if the most crank-shaped thing in all of Washington is D.C. and the most crank-shaped thing in all of D.C. is Anacostia, and what if Anacostia is GoGo's Bethlehem on the Potomac. Would that make Barry Farms a holy place, the most crank-shaped thing in the socket: a newborn foot?

94

Because you are African, really African, not from the Africa you were told you are from but a descendant of the natives of this land, a land whose pre Turtle Island name is lost—not from SE, SW, NE, NW, not a Gangster Chronicle or a Hillboy—you are caged and, among other things, the cage is covered, covered with souls, sounds and songs you cover, cover with your body, your whole body, every note, beat and sung-word a moment of possible nourishment, the choice to strengthen or weaken, from digestion to waste. Built into you to protect you from the cage coverers, the long roll of ancestry (not any of the short, watered down, disposable ones) like a mighty, percussive musculature of free radicals, keeps coming alive in you, again and again, noisily, here and there, all over this atmosphere.

95

There are things they use us for, reasons they need us to make money and things they say we are slaves to—like the rhythm. These are backwards expressions of us. They sound good but they are thin, a thin-o-cide. Moments like this GoGo could use a few really good GoGo Abolitionists (and not just a journalist or poet or someone from the Upper Crest of N.W.) but a hard-hitting GoGo Activist Party to guide the community toward counter-listening, counter-buying and counter-dancing not someone who will act as a cultural auctioneer but someone who will stand on the steps of the District Building and march the facts, one of which is that (when properly pocketed) the rhythm is actually a very ritualistic and powerful leader of the people!

96

I don't mind a mural or two but I won't help our jailers, not in poetry or photography, turn Chuck Brown into a community saint, something out of reach by future efforts, and something that diminishes his human complexity.

Patricia "Twink" Little, 2007

Copying Napoleon Bonaparte,
the Po Po
invaded GoGo,
  ooh la la la,
long before Crack
but both invasions
  were funded
by related parties.
The Pocket time-travels
  to become
the Socket. Tony Tee. The Socket
backs it on up
  to become
  the Pocket.
Both were once
    dirty buckets
that became Dope Jams.
Crank is the lever.
A winter coat of arms.
Valor and Sacrifice
guiding the way
to the shook one war,
  bomp bomp,
bronze and horseback,
across the bridge
to confront Virginia
but in the rush hour traffic
of history, Blue Eye
views the sky
as an ocean
and the cloudless, clout chasers of oxygen
between them
as yet another lie.

So they kept giving them things, small things, local things, things they never had, things like parks and murals and art openings even as it was becoming harder for them to hear themselves and feed themselves and clothe themselves and school themselves and health themselves, impossible in their own pockets, impossible and illegal, even as they were dying and being shut down and not reading and dancing at funerals and showing up for reunions, they kept giving them things, like mules hidden in stimuluses, everything they needed except the state of equal human-hood.

Once you were sold, branded and owned, profit was made off of you in order to tear down (or reset) your home and turn it into America. You were used to making numerous American, British and transplanted German families great. Now you buy from and vote for those same families, brand yourself, own a whole lot of nothing and profit is made off of you in order to continue the black magic that constructs your imprisonment. This was never a great nation for you. Your great nation has been your imagination, which is where all black noise, including GoGo, originates. Branding of any sort is an overseer's trick to keep you from becoming whole, to keep you from imagining a nation other than the current American one. The sad irony of GoGo "branding" is the same sad irony of Africans selling Africans into slavery, housing projects, and lifelong debt, all the results of having become prisoners of a war that has been taken off the books.

A crank note is the opposite of a car note.
A car note hurts the pocket.
A crank note locks it.

William "JuJu" House, 2007

Chuck Town

Charles Louis Brown
1936–2012

 Sell Chuck.
Buy Chucks.
One Chuck fits.

Lace up Liaison
gold Chucks,
  All Stars.

Chucks come in
  all pockets
not just Pops.

 High top,
low top, green
snake skin,

boot-length Chucks.
Battle of the
  Kicks—

 Kenboy,
 Suga,
 Milton,

 Kiggo,
 JuJu,
 Kwick.

Footlocker Chucks
may smell like
  condoms,

  but nunchucks
bow-leg the chain
    between Chucks.
Unlock Chuck. Chuck lock it.

Lorton Chuck up.
  Chuck so country.
Cost more

    to see a reformed Chuck
      than a pair
  of toe-guarded

Ex-converse Chucks.
  Women love
  a sweaty Chuck,

    Bamma and Show.
Shout like Lotto
      when Chuck sock*et*.

Rumors of a Chuck mural.
  A Chuck park.
Chuck jock it.

Chocolate City
Chocolate Chucks
by Chucky
  Thompson.

Win a Chuck
  Winnebago.
A Drama Cruise for two

  to Chuck Levins
    with Chucky Burwell & Boo.
Junk love Chuck.
  Chuck all a bucket got.

Win a week in Brad's
trumpet bag.
  Touch Cherie's sweet,

grown ass, Grown & Sexy keys.
Them play better
    in Chucks.

  Wet Chuck roaches
not the dry ones
Chuck left Reo.

Hustlers want a cut.
Chuck give 'em
  the bridge.

Chuck give 'em the shank
  but no gym
    shoe deal.

  Don't give a Chuck
how many times
  you saw Chuck.

More Bright
"Mighty Moe" Shorter
Moments in Chucks.

Chuck did push-ups.
Chuck gave Thanks. Chuck accepted Christ.
Chuck stopped fights.

Who baby dat?
Dat Chuck
Baby!

Wind me up Chuck!
Say What!?
Wind me
down
Brown!

Footz wore Chucks.
Sneakers talk
to pimps behind Chuck's back,

tie up two-faced
tennis shoe tongues
before they flap.

Elect Chuck.
Got Chuck. Got votes.
Now Listen! A tin,

toy wind-up Chuck,
already wound up.
"Wind me up
Chuck"

winds Chuck *up*
like a tradewind of well-tailored
wind-songs,

a tale of two Chucks,
Chuck Taylors,
wing-tipped. Breeze called Chuck

a Chuck never
too old to spill
his own too big

to refill Chucks.
9:30 Happy Birthday Chucks.
Not enough Chuck

then Chuck
enough Chuck tributes
to monument Chuck.

D.C. don't stand for
Dodge Chuck.
Run fast like Joe

in Chucks.
Any other way to go,
GoGo in Chucks.

Chuck fucks
with us.
We fucks with Chuck.

Even without Chuck,
Chuck band
still work,

still work, still work
  with Chuck
and Chuck ghost.

Scooby Chuck.
Picture Chuck taking
      a picture

of a Poet picture-taker.
I saw Chuck
in a hearse.

  Soul, reflection, search.
Chuck heard
my camera curse.
Just one more frame
  of flowers
      from Chuck
      for all of us.

Wind me up Chuck!
    Say What?
Wind me
      down
Brown!

Chuck Brown / The Godfather of GoGo, 2009

Stick Bag Perspective

Those years without books but with drums followed by those years without drums but with books, how to craft them into a third period of life that sang together? Without your father, you don't get the drums. Without your mother, you don't get the books although you were a pretty good book thief when you had to be and you had to be often. "Freeing slaves" you called it, and took the craft seriously, teaching friends.

In the thought-colonies of colleges, idea-hopping, bored, and calling home to find out how the shows went, how the culture was doing, but not having anyone to tell you or who could tell you, well, not to your satisfaction, not with flava, unless you asked them so many questions the expensive phone call became an interview. And not even one of your best friends who had the gift, the gift of mouth, and could talk, lead talk, and could move the crowd with meaning—even with his eyes closed, could tell you word-for-word or descriptively how the shows went without you because, perhaps, that friend did not read, did not have a relationship with the written word which enhances aspects of the logical mind and thus catapults the spoken beyond its casual self into a realm of constant composing, which made you think, "Where does the language in him come from? Is it created on the spot? Is it all an act, a theater of the senses, an already knowing or a live searching, verbally, through the physical texts of moving bodies?" Your new friends, though, thought they could do both (read and respond to the reading while writing, very modern, but not seeing the bodies the words came wrapped in). Your new friends knew nothing about your life as a pair of sticks, antennae and divining rod, one stick that was interested in poetic knowledge (not merely poems) and the other stick that was interested in scientific knowledge (not merely experiments), the real reparation, so you missed a home that did not miss you. And why would it?

You left behind so many important things, dead things still alive and living things not yet dead, formless beings—soft, unwrinkled and not yet corrupted by language, beautiful and soon to be, possibly, dangerous, victims and participants in the true purpose of the city: to turn breathing into stone and to tune that stone into a place of profit. What feeling is there to be felt between, as they say, "a rock and a hard place?" To the city, there were many of you. Too many. And the new place, not a hiding place, but the place where things were hidden, hidden then called disciplines of study, weren't any safer. History could hurt the mind, bury it, in any level of lies and attractive counter-narratives or events full of holes, holes able to please both sides of any conflict, while cementing the mind in a standstill of intelligent indecision. But always there was a temporary savior, the mother who sent money for books, the girlfriend who visited and brought GoGo cassettes with her no matter how many times you asked. But the very act of reading could erupt the heart into many things: shame, pain, pride, disgust, confusion, clarity and—like the drumsticks that your elbows, knees, shoulders and eyes had all battled each other to become—an instant feeling of liberation. That's all literacy was—same as dancing, same as loving, same as loss—another system of liberation with limits, another rule book of rudiments. If you were poor, however, once you conquered that level, the level of not being poor, another level of traps awaited you. One form. A Reform School. So it was important that you learned (at the right time in your life) to identify the energy field or integrity level of an idea, any idea, internal or external, as well as the patterned intentions of certain books and (of most importance) that you never allowed any doctrine, no matter the ism or rhythm, no matter the author or genre, to become a parent of your imagination at least not before you were confident enough to pull the mask off of the government and groupthink of grammar, achieving, at best, a skeptical solidarity with its many masters, meanings and measurements.

If you could do this, then, and only then might you, one day, articulate and construct, a new landscape of associations for what you heard in the pocket. Something of Proust, structurally, and something of what Donnell Floyd asked (at his last show) of his younger contemporaries, "the best to come test me," sonically, like a pocket poet, in the pocket, with a pocket full of photographs. Beings, beatings and beats all being named by the drum. A kit of planets. Ohm's law. An energy between one home and another, the voltage of duality. In the pocket, without any mind-altering substances, you could hear and feel much more than "twoness" and begin to fashion an existence and vocabulary that was as polyphonic as a phone call from the kidneys to the thalamus. The root word of number is numb. In the pocket, cognizant of an All, of the entire anatomy of the two aforementioned sticks. You felt able to be-in-earth, not just on the ground of the agreement of the age that bore you, but beneath whatever fiction you may have encountered, beneath essay, beneath poem, beneath the choreography and the drama of life-less art and art-less life, but mostly beneath the staccato, true and false, of the cage of categories and unfamiliar breathing that was alien to the order of your soul.

In the pocket, you felt natural and unarrested. In school, you felt the "poc" of pocket being turned into a person of color, a beatless identity cop.

Your new friends were like you, having their own drum-words and drum-work—the kind that was organized, the kind that had layers of definitions, the kind that can be tested…and yet, still, it fed you into a job, one with slightly better wings, perhaps, but they were unlike you, having the means to call upon the resources of family and support when the wells of their semester-to-semester drum-words and drum-work ran low or bored them. True of all of them except, perhaps, two, the two that always stood next to you like two timbales with a cowbell stand between them. All the time, constantly, you were a drum and it was never exhausting. Fearless, for the Collective, you were. You could go and go, bang and crash, roll and flow. The meaning of you and those you loved and who loved you was of a multi-interest-rhythmic-construct, every pore, camera eye and phone ear.

Years later, when you lived in San Francisco or daydreamt, percussively, while traveling up-high through Colorado, you wondered what was in the stained mountains, blood? The GoGo of Goethe came to mind, his theory of colors. What giant things, you wondered, had perished there? With one eye, squinting, from the Am I of Amtrak, they looked like pyramids, pyramids covered in former life, hardened life. You scribbled on a napkin: Drum-mountain / Pyramid-drum. The pyre of the idea burned a new mental rhythm into your understanding of the now. A smaller now that was once larger. History did not mean history anymore; it meant great as in Alexander the Great and Great meant Giant as in Goliath or Andre the Giant. Time to go and go and go into the geographic mouth of the first recorded, if not remembered, G. The vocabulary had changed to hide the size of the past. Uppercase with a skull, lowercase with a womb. You called her. You called him: We live in ruins. This place has been over. It ended a long time ago. It's all ruins. In need of sleep, a nap, the short story of sleep, you saved the napkin for later, knowing later is always moving away from an approaching of anything, in-tune and out of tune, the tone world. Not an enemy of flash but if you had your way, if you had larger hands, you would tune the landscape every time there was a general shaking of heads.

Tune, to own. Out of a disagreement with what you were seeing in the world versus what you were told was in the world, you'd refocus till the truth was an unbreakable lyric, the order of the words a proper tour guide across any map or cartographical lie, letting you know that something happened and was happening again, and that we were junk to someone—bad junk not good junk, and that the top of a conga (like a desert) was a scorched place where, perhaps, water had been moved and, percussively, removed.

Ty'kiyah and the GoGo Poster, 2012

John "Cabalou" and MeShell Ndegeocello, 1988

101

After the animal on the drums, the most animalistic thing in the pocket is "the moose call," the glide from one pitch to another which a conga player makes by sliding his finger and thumb across the surface of the skin of the drum. This form of mating call and party talk, a wet tone, is a tension stabilizer and a warning to partying elephants and donkeys that a percussive glissando might be forming, like a political animal trainer, a kranktrain, a solid pour along the concrete-coast, and curbed shores of avenues named after unrolled documents.

102

If you are wondering where Officer Robinson, our armed Badge of the Golden Age, was those nights when young folks were shooting and getting shot, well, I don't know but I do know that even though she may be gone, Miss Annie Mack needs a song. Together at the door, they were as different as a stack of contact sheets and a box of memory cards. Miss Mack, tough as color. Robinson, a black and white nightstick breaking spotlights. Captain Brady, let's start a band called The Miss Macks and sit on a porch with a bushel of crabs, red shells, as baritone ghosts clog the river's slick throat, deep-drowning the years the wrong pocket (not the people) made the revolver a lover, a raw shooter, shot in the raw of raw image.

103

In the future (which is really a PA tape of the past), the healthiest crank will be plant-based. No dairy. No red meat, only fish in the open high-hat on your face where there was once a mouth. Thick and crank-shaped like the Eastern Branch of the Anacostia River, you won't have to worry about your weight because you will be healthy, and you won't have to ask yourself, before the show, "Does the big white t-shirt I am wearing cover a well-fed, obese beat or a hollow and hungry, bloated bass drum?" Like a watcher who, in pursuit of weightlessness, has lost your way attaching wings to your waist, thy hell and thy health will have fallen away long before you leave the last stage of self and flesh.

104

The ancestors are taking their gifts back, rapidly, one human-instrument at a time. Maybe those gifts were promised to a more worthy recipient or to someplace more freestyle-divine than our patrolled pocket. There are signs of this everywhere, and you can feel it in the energy of those accustomed to the leavings, especially those who cannot cross due to the weight of being carried by the wrong cross.

105

The more familiar the groove became (to the band playing it) the faster and more "polished" it got. And by the time they took it to the studio, sadly, it was no longer spontaneous and had lost the living collaborative exchange that originally existed in the creative process; and all of the sound-nutrients that moved the crowd had become planned, fitted into their perfect slots and predictable. There is nothing livelier than a groove (a vein of growth) being born—the mistakes resisting refrain, the refrain disciplining formula, and the formula at the center of the form, making a pattern of itself just enough to become the last sun-on-the-ground, a finished song. All of this must be accomplished without losing contact with the ground. The ground is alive.

106

The decision is yours but before you vote, if you vote, do the pocket a solid and crank drunk the night before, District Line drunk. Teeter to the North, Maryland. Teeter to the South, Virginia. This is perhaps the only way to navigate all of the local, political spin that GoGo is forced to serve and swerve every election. Even the drinks at the bar contain spiked speeches. Vote for the candidate that does not keep track of the fingerprints on cassettes, the one who knows how to use his or her ear to twist a lens like cracking a safe. Being two fully-focused words, GoGo is partially two worlds—a party and a pulpit. Despite being exposed up on a cross in raggedy drawers, when you register crank, the crank of hardworking poor folks, the congregation cannot be fooled.

107

If your so-called PA recording, CD or tape, doesn't have any mistakes or natural human accidents on it then it ain't really a PA. The current structure of most supposed-to-be PA recordings is that of a glorified mixtape full of seamless transitions, a thing created away from the basic rights of the listener, music devoid of crowd participation, a copier of continuance. These restructured shows, or cleaned-up combined ones, turn our grooves into separate bills no one (on the dance floor) wants to pass or hear.

108

Somewhere the word GoGo is spelled with an abundance of utterances, and somewhere it will not stop until long after it reaches the 51 Syllables of Selfhood, not even if "the man" says it has to go 51 times, not even if security rolls up, 51 Deep. The word GoGo will just keep going, 51 times, beyond vote, veto, legislation, lobby, committee, community, out farther than the city limits of sovereign, into the content of country where it belongs.

109

Foot pedals should be sold in the grocery stores in Anacostia on a plate full of feet, the beater head wrapped in a felt mallet like bacon around a scallop on a rod-shaped metal shaft. Short loin, Teebone. The Big Chair should be replaced with an enormous replica of Heavy One's last drum seat.

110

One fine, redistricted day the last beatitude from the last beat from the last drop of pocket and drip of crank will finally reach us in our enclosed system of sound but for now, let us hope, it stays spot-lit years away. No camera holes, stars or starts, in the curtain of night. No final conflict of feet, stressed or measured, our beaten past an imperfect fit of planned locality. No Scorpio in the sky, stone cold, to beam down.

111

To know when to squeeze the cowbell for various tones. It's in the palm as much as in the pattern, not to mention the ability of dividing the body of the cowbell into a talk-that-talk caller ID of audio-anatomy, hard on the outside, hollow on the inside. The horticultural craft of being a bell gardener. Take time out for the handheld geography. Blow into the bell, rub the widening belly as if each finger is producing a tough prayer. Sticks taken orders from shoulders. Shoulders having those orders approved by eyelids clicking against the wet rims of a shiny caruncle.

112

No such neighborhood, not really, as National. No such office, not really, as official. No such obituary, not really, as original. No such lane, not really, as local. No such copyright, not really, as culture.

113

Tru Worshiperz

The twin spirits around the human spinal cord were tuned
by the star of the void
to lock in a coil
but along came the Crank of Service
to uncoil its song,
its vertebrae of tones,
its serpent of bones.

114

Folks like to say, "It takes a village to raise a child"
but the village has been compromised,
shot up, poisoned, polluted and pocketed,
real talk, now all it takes to raise a child is a yard, tiddy balls and dippers.

115

If you have heard "Say What!?" in your life more times than "I Love You" then you are probably crank-shaped and in need of the opposite of public, percussive assistance. You also probably possess a very critical brand of passion, one that wasn't flipped when everything else was flipped. You don't have to be triflin' to crank, but you do have to be hard on the outside and hard on the inside at least four nights a week. It's a weird form of togetherness and bang-together-touch, cranking, all you do is hit it, make hits and be hit especially if you want the city to listen.

116

The old city was addicted to the beat of togetherness, so the dealers of new things drugged them and their drums. A war was coming but not the war on drugs. The war that came was the war on drums. The new city is a dealer, an addiction-dealer, dealing eviction. The old things are most useful to the new things when they are being forced to leave. This used to be known as flight but that was before Ronald Reagan fired the air traffic controllers; that was before brothers started calling each other soldiers.

117

There is no such thing as an original song or an original son. All songs are cover songs, attempting to replicate the route of the sun covering the earth but no one song circles above us fast enough. This is why airplay was invented. The same is true of sons in relation to their fathers. The sun extends the circular route of the father creating the continuance of seed. Placed in the mouth, seed is note: eighth, quarter, half, whole. How the phases of the moon sound, it howls. Because the word can make flesh, the sun is the father of all songs. Songs already exist before we are used to pull them from air via talent, a recording of the word, the word made wax. To be on the charts is to be in an inferior constellation of hits. A hit is brightness fixed in place, a stuck star. Talent is a watered-down word for magic. Original is the ring of orbit, revolutions per minute. Songwriting is Sunrising.

Love and Sauce

CPU Re-loaded

Wrists talk,
palms speak,
arms that agree
with the thick skins
of all eight skulls.
Smack, crossover, smack.
More than speed
passes between them,
more than the basic
"what's up"
of breathing hands,
what it all means is definition-less,
a physical vision
 of local brotherhood.
All ten unified fingers
originating
from the knees
up through the elbows
where the bones
that contain the Savings
& Loans of joints
become the grammatical
accounts of heartbeats and hours in a conga,
what we can't withdraw
  unless we thumb roll
        and inhale
 all of the years
the pocket fed their ears.
Envelope licks.

Saliva, line scrawl, stroke.
Out of equal respect,
one laughs at the other,
     smiles hiding
the secrets of the slick moves
we miss just
being listeners.
LP: Locked Pocket.
  Pop.

119

Where are the whistle blowers, the go-betweens, the non-major chords, the
ones ready to move the pocket away from corruption and corruption away
from the pocket with dog training whistles, a sound only the "locked" can
hear, the ones with train whistles along the railroad tracks, tin and metal
pea whistles, steam whistles, soul-searching whistlers, famous for, "…any
kind of whistle just blow," wind master and tornado whistles, solid brass
pipes, finger whistles and taxi whistles, the magpie chatter and blue jay
call of bird whistles, slide whistles, the new movement of party whistles,
plastic Day-glo referee whistles, all aboard the next express of whistles to
be blown, three generations of po tow mack tones!

120

The word "GoGo" looks and sounds like a balanced utterance, like a
community of syllabic equality, like a respectful union of double sameness
but it is not and never was, so don't believe what you hear at reunions
and funerals. True unity cannot be found at 2 a.m. in the parking lot of
a Wing Spot, peace. Often, though, one "Go" will switch camps after
disagreeing with the other "Go." In extreme cases a fight will break out
and the hyphen will become a knife. I remember one particularly violent
night when one half of the word heard the pocket say something about
resistance and art, and the other half beat itself to death because its heart
could not handle resistance or art.

121

for Carlos "Los" Chavez

The Word Ingredients of Skillet

ill
ilk
tell
let
kill
till
ski
skit
tisk
'tis
sit
like
list
lest
skill
Skillet
Elks
Ellis
Eli
No Skittles
sike
sill
still
is
Ike
set

sell
slit
silt
silk
kit
kite
kilt
tie
tile
lil'
lit
lite
lie

122

It which serves the city or the state cannot also serve the People unless it is, first, able to convert the People and its cultural product into a product of the State or convert the interest of the State into a useful tool of the People. The latter is rare and requires a savvy radicalism not glimpsed, locally, since the early administrations of Marion Barry. Crank is at the crossroads of converter and being converted.

123

The Freak-a-deke Zone

Where all things return to being one thing. Zero to one, no further. The 10 that got turned around while dancing with itself. No number, no integrity of integer. Zero makes no rule for 0 nor does nothingness. It gives itself away because it is a part of everything, an All. Nothing leaves. Go and Go that sacrifices a piece of itself to grow contains God. Go and Go that holds on to its whole self does not. Soon the entire outer construct will be gone only to be found in the electric eye of Wings World.

No place out cranks / cranks out Carry Outs like Anacostia and before it was anglicized, ghetto-fied and demonized the name Anacostia meant "Trading Village" and the Nacotchtank ate fish from the river, and were healthier than the incoming settlers who founded nothing in this land but the earliest forms of genocide. If you walk into a small, dirty restaurant (with a bulletproof barrier between you and the food and where "Lock It" is being played,) run, because the Carry Outs are there to take you out and to cleanse the banks east of the river. Revitalization is not All4U.

125

You don't have a soul.   A soul has you.

It's the same with crank.

You are not cranking.   Crank be you ing.

Tylisa "TyTy Vicious" Brown and Leonard "Daddy-O" Huggins, 2010

The Cowbell King

Lloyd Ashley Pinchback
1948–2020

Held upside down,
 and played low,
I don't think
 he ever raised it higher
than his open heart-shaped face
   or his
   closed fist
   shaped heart.
O earth salt
 of the poorer regions
where the folks that live close
   to the ground
   could experience it.
Nor did he ever bang it,
 like neophytes do,
near the library drum of his Congressional ear,
 not even to deafen Judas,
                not even
         to depopulate
   the pocket's bar
of drinkers of justice
 which is why no photographer,
   camera-wise
          enough to sync
pigment, hue and cry,
ever needed a flash

to chart the royal resonance
of his signature
sun king-to-sun skin
inner kinships. A performance-worth of morning
　　in the profile,
　　side view from the flute,
　　stick against cow,
　　as legally blind
as the calm, patterned reign
　of available light
flowing through the arteries
　of the Burgundy Room,
the amount of oxygen
　　in each vessel
　　determining
　　the integrity
　　of the blood cells.
The blood cell are notes.
A percussive a thing as a thunderstorm
　　in a rotunda
　　in a stone circle
at a roundtable of churches
falling through
the showers of Category 5 Cathedrals,
new life
　hitting itself
　　to disguise itself
　　　　as the end of life
　　in a new skin
to tenderly begin.

Lloyd Ashely Pinchback, 2012

Stick Bag Perspective

The cowbell, being a skull-belly, being a library, being a portal, either, speaks to you or from you as if more than one of you (possibly even three of you) were playing it at once: you making it copy itself, you making it mistake its past for its present, its present for its future, you making it correct itself—not the standard hearing lens, not the limited seeing limbs, not slaughtered livestock on a gelatin plate or a camera hanging from the photographer's neck like a cowbell full of film. It, both mouth and crown, going from hot to cold in the grasp of a groover, and (depending on the exposure and how long the lens stays open) ringing like the lips of sound holding together an urban rainbow. Hands have faces. Palms, grooves, lines in skin, ley lines, alignments. Maps make a better grasp. City, pattern. Motor vehicles beat the pavement until the Young Impressions in the skyways can feel the rhythm. Atmospheric exhaustion. Long before Climate Control, there was Cowbell Control. Cold bells and warm bells, warm hands and cold hands, hollow bells whose ringing could destroy a civilization.

Crank Geoengineering, a resonance.

Lower the cowbell like a camera and you will see the masonry wall of the tidal basin beneath the cherry blossoms. Beat, Lens, Matrimony (BLM). As if it, and both moods and modes, were being pushed through the echo system that often followed a wave of content and the crossing (from one side of ground to the other) what we call the bridge or the bride of government. Echoplex, ecosystem, solar plexus. A live stream stemmed in the mystery of no conversation between ponds, no pocket. No pocket, no ticket cop. Poplar Point, where Moe palmed a plastic bucket like a miniature drop shaft. A drum pad cannot help improve the traffic between the dealer and the user unless the runner is cognizant of the layers above his lane. One must be able to hear, without the small scale of ignorant frustration, the levels of operation in order to appreciate the form of the high rise in every cowbell. As if, the body of the bell, this empty tenement, were a part of the building—or a brick banged into place, and, perhaps too, the fastest changer of ideas, structural ideas, within the whole per-cussin' community, the high-speed concentration of essentials, cemented in essence.

Per cussin': Fuck it. Per-cussin': Don't nobody want to hear that shit all the time. Per-cussin': Damn, that's some good ass crank curving into our realm, into our rhythm, crawling and kicking like the quality of the percussive conversation taking place behind the back of the beat till the backbeat, in the percussive talk of people who per cuss, reconstructs a human drum talk of spittle spraying a one-world cap, a dome, into place.

Fort Circle Park: Fort Stanton, Fort Mahan, Fort Ricketts, Fort Benning, Fort Chaplin and Fort Davis. A cool breeze at Breeze's. A Hollywood Breeze in D.C. Where the workers went, the transporters, the Metro Club, that's where this improved perspective first gave and got show. You already know…because you are a Know Nothing. You already know the ceiling was low. You already know there aren't any photographs from that day, know-it-all of nothing. You know, Know-Nothing, I could be making all of this up and shaping it with crank, with banging language and a guttural nod to Seamus Heaney, so that something in the natural-knowing, in the discovery, is convincing and a catalogue even as it is being invented, warmed-up, so warm it's humid. To be governed by the mentality of a rude database. Page cold as marble, white blocks. No crank in Luxor, Vegas or Egypt. Took in everything R.A. Schwaller de Lubicz said about "pavement as mosaic" and heard, instead, "mosaic as music." Like Googie, my ears convert everything to balance. Ernest Kroll here speaking: "How shall you act the natural man in this/Invented city, neither

Rome nor home?" Vacca is cow in Latin. Bell is tintinnabulum. Vacca tin tinn looks like Vatican. Vaccinae from the adjective vacinnus means of or relating to cows. Latin Percussion. That's something you, and you, Left Sticks and Right Sticks, already knew.

Not a single scenario, overnight or over easy,

includes a plan for owning a club.

There weren't any breezes, not really, in Breezes, only levels of history folks like Moe Gentry did their best to master. The thermometer of human listening has not been properly written about because science is still a skeleton. Ever see a drum set minus the tom toms and cymbals? Just stands, a pedal and a seat. Another example of Know-Nothingness: Breezes was the opposite of The Ice Box. Double function. The air had to bend time, through the front door, to get to the stage area, then reverse and bend time again to get to the bar. That's how we discovered what time it was, what time is, what time "it" always is…all the times all the time… even when there is not any time or time to do anything. You want to play cowbell, if so, know this: You don't need either of me. You don't need a stick. Emphasis on the typical, non-practical hints. Hits. Know this: time inside the cowbell is not the same as time outside the cowbell. Depth of field has limitations, within the frame, discontinuing time. Depth of time is frameless.

The images inside the cowbell are not the same as the images outside the cowbell. The walls, interior or exterior, are usually black or silver. What kind of entrance, what kind of exit is the mouth of sound? Diversion sewers are best kept near the river. Hains Point, a strip of land between the Washington Channel, the Georgetown Channel and the Potomac. There's a golf course there, one I can see from any stage. Mound site or Sound site? One is ideal for snapshots, the other provides advantages of the large scale of view, so you better learn to squeeze and un-squeeze all three sound zones, river tunnel too.

Before it is beaten out of them, cowbells possess invisible bicameral minds and a way of connecting to the electrical circuitry of subterranean infrastructure. Between the green Trigonometry book, my Speedo trunks and cap and a Carl Sandburg book of poems, mine made my bookbag twice as heavy but I never showed the cold, loud thing to anyone at Dunbar.

Chris "Rapper Dude" Black, 2009

126

There is a conservative party within GoGo, a locked-in old guard of memory-makers, holding the keys to the history (like jingle jangle) over the bouncing heads of the younger and freer radical party. They want the per cuss sons and daughters to know what they know, respect what they respect, and to pass qualifying exams at their grand old feet but the problem is that the youngins' see their old feet as broke, broken and Baroque, as things neither to be or beat.

127

While the teacher tried to lead talk through social studies, we beat on this:

128

It's Official. Crank's Government Name is GoGo.

129

A hole in the pocket, something ripped from its pore, a sore cloth.
Helium and healing for the muse of song, balloons for the missing son.

Unlike an antithesis in need of a thesis some tromboyer would be nice, not just as the property of intellectual property or f lever problem-reaction-solution, but as Crank's sliding syntax, a silver-plated piece of mouth against taxation without representation. Water key, bell lock and ferrule.

131

for Derek "Redfootz" Freeman

The human heart is a red foot pumping red music, not blood. The red set around the body stains the ground, stains it with breathing and the wounds of home rule, leaking. A red foot pumping red music, surgically, removes the stitches between Statehood and the union, the union of hills infested with seats. Not all of the bodies standing over our bodies are ours; some of them belong to laws, laws disguised as morals because anyone with a compass is trying to control you with magnetic rhetoric. A red foot pumping red music, not blood, already in the rotation of native souls, the bond (in concrete) we leave behind.

132

The scheduled battles, the ones wrapped in organized hype, the ones between pockets that like lint but dislike lining, the ones that show off and decide nothing while we stand around and watch, the portable ones with too many participants who all smack with the same degree of likeness, the ones that reduce the language of ancestral resistance to a competition for money, the ones that are intimidated by "Carnival," don't recall "Festival Style" and have never heard of "Second Line," the promised ones that protect us from the constant attacks of stillness by carrying messages of survival between neighborhoods, villages, wards, quadrants and crews, the ones who mark themselves safe long before the bridge is blown, the ones who (after a decent work week) get online and go live just to let everyone know they made a few extra time Fugio cents.

GoGo with nowhere to go,
um bop bop,
is still homegrown
GoGo,
but GoGo
that sounds
like it's been somewhere,
berro e sombaro
 has a hard time
  of coming home
and finding
a job and a crowd.
SayNoMore.
Once there was
a be bumpin' way
of growing at home,
yuck yuck yuck yah
but it was the same way
of not being
able to grow
anywhere but home.
On my mind.
D.C. has an uncalled 4 way
of being closed,
cliquish and addicted to the familiarity of family,
known faycez,
often dissin' any outsider
or an insider
with a wider vybe.

134

To be free in front of the national monuments, not behind them.

135

Some pockets, like bank accounts, are either emptier or fuller than others. It does not depend on how many hands using sticks, hitting skins, or holding instruments reach in. It depends on the blend, the rhythm-rate of different types of interest, the timing of the loan, and the grammatical ease and entering of the savings passed from one broke, break down to another. Like a generous ATM machine being frisked at 2 am, the pocket knows when to groove to set the clock back and when to crank to move the clock forward. The great thing about Bounce clock is its impatience, the way it does not waste any time retiring slummin' elders.

136

for John "Stinky Dink" Bowman

Crank is freedom, the feet of locked elements freed from the fear of local graves and local gravity. A new dimension, both inner and outer space, beyond the short-arm reach of temporal recognition, beyond the licked-fingering of fake fiscal gesturing. When we turn our pockets inside-out bending the contents of time with our bodies of struggling sound, the pocket-vocabulary, a tight unit of verse reversal, beats at the speed of rickety raw lyric-intention energized by the supporting syntax of sensitive synthesizers, faster than being locked-up in the artificial light of fame and brighter than the spark of life, the word made mic, that becomes a rally against the systematic limitations placed on crank rap.

137

The stick is the greatest cowbell player of all time.

I, Pocket
may be just
a container
 but by the time
I get some
content
I will be
 a continent,
and the way you
exploit me,
deeper and deeper,
 will move
 me more.

U, native
Washingtonian,
used to be
 my cowbell,
the loudest
open mouth
in the city,
 hand-held not
  hand over.
Crank poured from concrete.
Concrete
hardened crank.
 Now U
 just a Street,
a Club U.

Speaking of the onomatopoeia of selective beat breeding and the urban agricultural revolution in the drum which contains a donkey in the kick and the comedy of physical farming in the broke and hungry dance of raw materials, the fields, that have made sustainable GoGo look and sound country ever since the age of simple digging sticks and hoes, many of who want their "hee" to be flat and their "haw" to be fat, domesticated, and deeply beneficial, with much love and respect, to the laws of local popularity and selection. Translation: Hey, don't sleep on that.

140

Capitalism is not crank-shaped. You can play for pay all you like but the true essence of crank, the need to avoid and under-rhythm the machine, will never be satisfied (fully) by money or recognition. The shapes of crank have more in common with the individual Woke Health Organs (of the body) than the World Health Organization, or any social criteria or curriculums of wellness. Ever notice how good you feel in the pocket— bounce, groove or bucket? Anti-pharmaceutical, crank is the height of holistic healthiness in the Industrial World.

141

There are no strangers in nature. A groove is built the same way the body is built. It imitates the process of Creation but is ignorant of the process and must search the spiral ritual of the spirit. The spirit is spatial not merely the spit and spat of Spoken Word. The hip bone connects to the thigh bone and the thigh bone connects to the leg bone, so although Hip Hop may have the advantage of narrative, lyric content, over GoGo—but Funk, the life force of the physical, human body working out to achieve its aim, is the advantage GoGo has over Hip Hop. The funk of Hip Hop is flat. The funk of GoGo is round fat. Think of these modes of a genre as vessels. Mics don't drop like meteors. Meteors drop like mics. Hip Hop has had better Government Schools and Government support groups than GoGo, better entertainment handlers.

The District Building, 2009

142

Eye Socket

The photographer's dream GoGo would have the band playing on a glass stage, so that the photographer could capture the band from underneath. The monitors would each contain a large format Polaroid camera with timers set to shoot every 51st cymbal crash. There would be cameras facing the audience attached to the back of all of the frontline microphones. The conga skins, like sensitive lens, would focus when fingered and zoom when smacked, and the rototoms would f-stop when twisted. The new sound of the foot pedal would be the sound of a shutter, manually posing the groove, while the snare advanced every leg (on the floor) like the lever that cranks film through the club's darkroom of nondigital bodies. All of which, of course, could be controlled from a board (in the head) similar to a PA System, small and non-threatening though, and known as the Eye Socket.

143

To destroy the content of Crank, trace the shape of the black body with white chalk (as if making an arrest) then call it art.

144

All cameras crank but the crank must be willing to expose itself to multiple formats. Format is the form matter takes to become material. Crank has no alma mater. In the hands of a former pocket maker, the camera can tell the difference between types of crank. There are eyes in the pocket, analog and digital. Film loves the frontline. Digital loves the backline. A camera in the crank is just a way of stopping the homicides of time.

145

If the main ingredient in crank is protest, "Lock it, lock it," parts of the pocket would not behave like cops.

A pocket blocker is someone who likes the beat but not the peeps. A police blotter is something that likes the peeps and knows how to beat.

Being "in the pocket" has just as much to do with "the pocket being in you" as you being in it. Inside the pocket you are valuable and you can feel the percussive worth of self, every level and layer of life (especially love and loss), flowing into the from-of-you. The pocket inside you was always there, yearning to be heard into, long before you were ever filled or emptied by the touch-like reach of need.

Some Bounce Beat bands have a dying dream that won't lay down. Other Bounce Beat bands have a lot of wide-awake beats still learning to rise. I don't have a dream but I do believe Crank woke us.

The myth that GoGo needs help creates the need in GoGo for help. The qualities of Hell are hidden in many dens and in many needs. "When you walk in the door and you come to GoGo, say what, hello hello hello!"

Crank ain't two-faced and crank ain't clock-shaped. My pocket ain't be-got no weapon because my weapon ain't be-got no hole-less pockets. Crank ain't full of votes. I did see a few Campaign Block Captains at block parties but not a single baller stuffin' ballots. When crank won, it lost. When crank lost, it lost. Too many non-cranking delegates. Time to bounce.

The First Lady of GoGo

Maiesha Linda Rashad
2020

Some hugs
never end for opening.
They merely
become mature closure,
stages of embrace,
not clients of distance,
never, not in a lifetime,
a single inhuman moment of pulling away
        from
the desires of grown folks.
The desires of grown folks,
lonely, yet alive,
in the night of nothing.
In the night of nothing,
it's any time you set the sky-clock,
the body clock,
the world clock to be,
including the time between time,
the time of birth, no time,
or half-past the last time
you had a real reason
to treat yourself like an adult
and go out and be out
        out,
        out,
        out again,

with a voice and a few friends.
With a voice and a few friends,
Seventies-dressed,
in the name of Resurgence,
of night air entering the stomach,
your last name Rashad,
a Renaissance of hip birds,
a musical appetite created by the local oxygen
that once made men walk like sideburns
and every inch of a woman,
a monument,
 worth standing in line for,
   surrounded by friends not flags,
     back when our city
       was a village.

Maiesha Linda Rashad, 2012

Stick Bag Perspective

The sun did not bounce. It launched off of the superstructure so I could not shoot as freely as I wanted. It was one of those Washington, D.C. summer days when the sky looked like a mixture of light blue and white, milky marble, one of those days when the oxygen between you and the sky was already, invisibly, wet before it made you, visibly, sweat. A deodorant day, emphasis on rant and door. Nothing worse than entering an air-conditioned building through spinning doors accompanied by a stranger or two with funky arms or too much cologne or perfume. The odor freezes but before it freezes, a cymbal crash with a kickdrum punch under it occurs in both nostrils, sometimes rising up behind the eyes.

Most of my time was spent positioning and repositioning myself trying to avoid the glare of white shirts. Unless you are perched above it all or have access to a unique view, there is no way to photograph The Hill, without an access pass to the private halls and corridors of power, and not have it appear like a series of inferior postcard observations, so best to break the photographic chore into smaller exercises of interests and concentrate on the miraculous accidents of light and human behavior to make it interesting.

Walking from the Botanical Gardens to the Capitol Building to the Supreme Court Building took less time than I imagined. I arrived forty-five minutes early all of which was eaten, easily, by the wide current of taxis, tour buses, cars and public transportation of upper Independence Avenue. Unless I am able to get close to a subject, it is difficult to get photographs that do not include trees, cars, buses. A man sitting with a statue of Jesus. I got close (or so I thought) but later when I saw the image, I was not close enough. I had a Leica R4s with me that day that had a slight light leak in it from being dropped, more than once, in the GoGo. The back of the camera was taped with black electrical tape and this made the process of changing film slower.

Former Soul Searcher, Lloyd Pinchback, was several minutes late and I thought, for a moment, that he might not show but there he was: arms, belly, glasses and cap, bright as the sun that challenges the sun, motioning me through the entrance and escorting me through security. Wise of him to choose the Library restaurant for lunch. No recollection of what we ate but I do recall that he let me choose our seats. I chose a seat in the window overlooking Independence Avenue with a view of The Thomas Jefferson Building whose architecture I had been fascinated with for years. Like many other buildings in Washington, it did not look like it belonged in Washington unless, of course, you accepted the official story of Washington.

Lloyd was very easy to talk to and, like me, seemed to have a mind that was always in more than one place at a time, including the realm of mindlessness, silence. I made sure to ask a lot of questions about his life—growing up in D.C., coming to music, the early Soul Searchers. And although talking about Chuck was unavoidable, I was careful not to make the mistake of asking questions that were more about Chuck than him, because I was genuinely more interested in the Lloyd's mind and story than the Chuck story which I had heard so many times I was beginning to doubt it.

Lloyd answered my questions unguarded and openly. I explained bits and pieces of my life while returning the conversation to his. He asked how long I had been writing poetry and I explained ever since I stopped wanting to be a football player, a Sayers, on the field in a green and white

Kingsman Boys Club uniform at the age of 13 in 1976, probably against Wheaton, Bethesda or Olney. In one of those games, it rained and, instead of scoring six times, I fumbled six times. To became a lyric writer, I had to stop wanting to be a lyric runner. If, as Muhammad Ali said, "writing is fighting," then being a percussionist is also being critic, why not, the school desktop was my first drum and page. I should have taken a photograph of Lloyd's face. It was pure gentle poker meets the pocket.

He stopped a few of my questions from entering his mind, wanting to save those answers for the book he was writing. Wow, he was writing about his life! I was happy to find someone else who was also writing about their experiences in GoGo.

He asked about photography and, because of where we were, I told him about the time I met the poet Howard Nemerov (1988), compliments of my Aunt Doris who worked at the American Folklife Center in the Jefferson Building, and how years later (2006) after my first book was published, I gave a reading at the Fine Arts Work Center in Provincetown, Massachusetts with Amy Arbus, the daughter of photographer Diane Arbus. I told him that I did not realize that Howard Nemerov and Diane Arbus were siblings, poetry and photography, until Amy asked to photograph me after our event.

I did not really answer Lloyd's question but I did "worry" the area of it.

I was trying to say that poetry handed me photographer like running the football handed me poetry but it came out like a sequel to an answer and not an answer that could stand on its own.

I was nervous, happy to be in the company of a former Soul Searcher, and already (in my mind) trying to figure out the best way to photograph him on such a bright day in the sun that affected his sight, made him squint and withdraw his eyes.

Soul Searcher Donald Jerome Tillery, 2012

Reunion

Sometimes when band members,
like male divas
or river branches,
no longer get along,
they scatter into related camps,
the same as the stars that fall to Earth,
the ones that become rocks,
and the same as the stars
that move through the heavens,
the ones that become lights,

each luminous body taking with it
the civil war of local audience,
a loyalty as divisive as bragging rights and favoritism,
the bone fragments of homegrown Crews
or organ donors on opposing shores,
fists cocked at each other,
making humidity with drums,
the attitude sickness
that becomes altitude,
conflict, and big-headedness,

the internal split caused by ego,
the eternal verb of GoGo
growing as the groove grows,
ego grooving to ego grooving to ego,
offstage cliques determined
by the selective prejudices of upbringing and talent level
not by maturity and true friendship,

fangs hidden in the vamp of songs
pretending to soothe before they soar,
the formula of personality

built into every performance
like the lack of harmony in money,
no three-pocketed dollars
ever agreeing to save or spend alike,
certainly not the so hard to handle pioneers,
cashed, caught and compromised
in the stubborn cages of their own styles
refusing to change or make change for anyone
until the worked walls

of their wallets are threatened
or a popular member or two is murdered or dies
then the percussive trends of youth
are employed, once again,
to re-up the backline's war on rigor mortis,
old beefs churned to cheddar,
venues with guts, gutted, an updated logo,
legacies and legends rebranded,
city-allegiance, a t-shirt marked by three stars,
an Equals Sign, a map of the District

cut-out and forced into a D
like a raggedy audition,
a C like a horizontal key hole,
reputations sprinkled with the noble seasoning
of revisionist hood memory,
the only place where the past
can be polished and dragged through the mind

like an obituary of greatest hits
on a setlist of recognizable corpses,
every celebration a cemetery of time,

gravestones thrown at the glass houses
where the bones of former band members are stored
and summoned from the casket of cassette
to the burning cremation of CDs
where a live reunion,
despite the hustle of promoter hype,
is just another one of Rome's resting places
of onstage spiritual unrest,
ritualistic, recorded and remixed,
an improbable pain-sweetened perfected togetherness,
locked into the same resurrected pocket

of time travel as prayer
and the fire of future anniversaries
because a foundation for icons,
even one with exposed roots,
is more profitable than icon resurrection,
the mural gods of agreeable GoGo
put in place to keep the unruly natives emotionally in check
like the bridge of personalities
no manager was ever able to cross
without, first, covering the basement windows

and the positive vibes of home life,
good credit and social standing
from all the late nights and hours of standing
outside the fabric of drama
like a skilled referee of raw ambition,

pretending not to be a well-spoken,
protective brick in the necessary wall
between the band and the world
damn-near an extra parent,
street-wise in a suit, go-between & role model,

the one who pays for studio time,
that necessary tutelage of discovery,
where the headaches rebegin
and the energy, booth-controlled, is not the same as a live performance,
tracks compressed by rules,
first released single, although successful, a roster killer,
Producer intentions vs band vision,
the casualties of choices buried in the session
like a record of the umbilical cord
between hearing and the engineer: snake cables,

a box with sixteen channels,
quickly bounced files, digital bodies,
taken advantage of by the full support of apparitions,
ghosts & spirits, the evaporating appreciation
of replacement lineups
no medley can fully embody
not even during a night of multiple fights.
Know them by their reunion uniforms,
syncopated and matched like they've known each other
longer than they've known each other,

long before the lifeline of going live,
long before the lie of life
and the bylaws of longevity
—so many musicians let go, recalled, then let go again,

the cycle of making a thing think in terms
of forever instead of free,
one "Go" for source, family.
And the other "Go" for resource, nostalgia,
two different aspects of the show,
one being the unprofessional selfishness
  of stage selfies,

an individual's spotlight of vanity,
satellite perspective,
and the trap of repeating
yet another infinite event with good-looking people
all sealed off from
their own tomb of logos
by the winged symbology of identifiable energy
and the orbiting grooves of gravity,
too many former stars,
teams and squads, dying for a place

in the future in a mural.

The One On One Roll

"James Funk made you mad and it became a hit."
Andre Johnson

Because dreaming and breathing are one, because breathing and drumming are one, one road, the most recognizable beat (place to "be at") in GoGo is also the most deceptive one. It sounds simple. It looks simple, beginner-simple, like an easy beat but it's not a beat; it's a roll. All hands no feet, a ride and a climb from the snare up around the high tom, mid toms then down to the floor tom. All drummers are travelers. All rolls are roads. Nine steps and a slick two-stick hiccup in the middle. A kick to the bass drum before opening the high-hat to begin, to bang and beg in.

Quietly cue before you queue Quentin. The best song intro in all of GoGo, the one every drummer thinks he can hear and thinks he can play but they always leave out the attitude, the context, and the tension between Funk and Footz, grown siblings, between men with a loud silence between them, between brothers who can't help but be brothers, the

> "I don't really want to play it
> but Imma play it
> for my brother
> because I love my brother,"

the

> "Imma make him play it
> till he gets it right
> because I hear something new
> and the audience
> likes it."

All this because his brother got on his nerves, because his brother kept asking for a roll, so he gave him a roll, not a real one, a mock roll, a being-funny-on-the-drums roll, the stick-sequence a younger brother gives his older brother when he doesn't want to be bothered, because it's not cool to beat him up, a signifying roll that would become a signature, a template, and a local rite of passage for other drummers. Lore: Funk made him do it, made him shed the clutter, including the excess bad blood, the fluid-it, and the memory of those times when human weakness interfered with family, with togetherness. Listening to the roll makes me wonder who was apologizing to who, the brother who asked for the roll or the brother who responded? Over time, the apology was perfected, publicly, in performance. One brother calling for our participation in the acknowledgment of the other brother's passing. That's why we put our hands in the air, the invisible ground of everywhere. Footz used to get us ready for the air. Air is water, thick oxygen. We breathe-in Footz when we put our hands in the air. Never forget. We put our hands in the air because Footz forgave his brother. Footz moves through the air in the roll his brother asked for. Clean air (between siblings) is rare. The roll moves through us. We travel with it, with them. Footz introduced us to the air we put our hands in. And before he died, he forgave his brother. Funk is for never get. Footz, forgiveness. Sticks in the casket. Resurrection, roll.

James "Jas. Funk" Thomas, 2010

Donnell Floyd, Frank Marshall, Mark Lawson, Brad Clements,
Kenny Gross and Kwanice Jackson, 2012

II

Music was originally brought to Washington by the government.

WPA Guide

The Saga of Lee Webster

A Photographic Triptych, 2007

There are many Washingtons, but one of my favorite things to do in the Washington that I am not from is stand on the backside of the U.S. Capitol Building and stare over the oval reflecting pool across the National Mall toward the Washington Monument, Lincoln Memorial and Arlington National Cemetery. On a clear day, from one hill to the other, you can see the edges of Arlington House, the Robert E. Lee Memorial. The mansion is described as the first example of Greek Revival Architecture in America. Even as a teen, studying D.C. History, I wondered who would want to revive Greece in America and as a young adult, with camera-enhanced eyes, I wondered, if true revivals and renaissances only occurred after resets or the cyclical fall of civilizations.

Standing on the steps, I am often reminded of "The Fall of Rome" by W.H. Auden. His meter comes to me, as if a ray of oral-frequency from the eye in the capstone of the Washington Monument, bloodshot and wrinkled as the age he left behind.

From that view you are the original ground zero, a Giza, the dome of the Capitol, and you are the place of the origin of avenues. A statue of a woman with a sword stands on your head. You are crowned by her and you have your eye-choice of Smithsonian Buildings, large art galleries, and various other memorials to focus your far-sightedness on.

Focusing stops vision.

The sun was turning everything with water in it into heat and that made people, without any idea where the hate was coming from, momentarily hate the sun and hate each other. It made them cranky. Humans have no idea that they have a hand, a bodily hand, in the creation of humidity. But like the rest of us, the sun just wants to eat and drink and needs us to eat and drink to accomplish this.

The sun eats of us and we eat things with the sun in it. That is true nourishment. The more sun in our food the better.

Overlooking one side of the city from on-high was like traveling three roads, all taken, at once. I did not have to engage the false regret of Frost's poetic setup. The passport of sight, of real sight, not imagined seeing, was mine to try out in multiple directions; and neither tired feet or heat calling home evaporating body fluids, the swim of expiring souls, could prevent me.

A craving like rain stabbing a living valley.

A craving for sushi and samosas.

While walking from Capitol Hill to North Capitol Street I saw several homeless Dantes and placed them on film.

I love photographing the exterior of Union Station but whatever it was, it was not a train station. From the outside looking in, you could tell that someone had put a train station in a building that was once something else and then, over time, updated the train station. At least that's what my camera-creative eye saw. Olmsted's shade, his law. I sat, facing east, on a bench in Lower Senate Park. Louisiana Avenue leaned toward me as if it were trying to tell me something about the gardens. Apple juice in a clear jar the shape of an apple.

Camera bag next to me like a companion. Splash!

A shirtless black man ran into the reflecting pool. Power plant,

Roman thermal bath.

Shallow, rectangular. I stopped eating.

The sun kept eating. Seemingly, hungrier than it was at noon, seemingly higher, but I really couldn't say for sure unless I blindly trusted my eyes which placed everything within my field of vision on a curve without showing me the curve. Wheel of vision?

The man in the pool lifted his legs, placed his arms around them, making with his body the universal position of comfort, of chillin', of being relaxed.

He looked like what Rodin's The Thinker should have looked like had he not been posing for a sculptor. I've never been sure of that as the best position for thought. It looks like it lost something, maybe wings, or failed a test or just arrived in a new world. It looks post-plague and like he's wondering where everyone else has gone.

Though odd to see on the Capitol Grounds, the man who ran into the reflecting pool looked happy to find water and sitting there he seemed to only exist between thoughts, his and mine. Did anyone else see him? It was hard to tell. Horseback officers frequently passed and there were people walking through the park. Between my thoughts, between the sushi and the samosas, I thought, "This is incredible, folk-federal surreal."

If I walk a short distance to the northern border of the pool, I will be able to photograph him sitting directly under the dome of the U.S. Capitol Building. But surely he would move or get upset or turn away or curse me before I had a chance to take the photograph. I walked to the end of the pool, centered myself and photographed him in the lap of the neoclassical giant in Olmsted's landscape and then so as not to be greedy or too much of an exploiter, I walked back to the bench.

Time, with small birds in its face of a mouth, crawled the lower sky.

The birds said nothing but the witnessing leaves of the trees in the park were made greener by summer.

I ate again. First time in my life that six pieces of an avocado roll and two pieces of ebi took longer than five minutes to eat.

Distant car sounds, a tour guide on a tour bus and still the language of legs moving through water, like sticks writing across the surface of a sheet of Remo mylar, was able to reach me. The man in the pool moved. He turned over on his belly, his head and shoulders being the only parts of his body not underwater, up and down like he was doing aquatic pushups. I walked back to the edge, shot him again. "Are you ok?" Nothing, not a word, just a sculpture: Black Swan in June. Before the bench called me back, I photographed him again—a few frames of film, several files of digital—but this time from the side of the pool, I didn't take my eyes off of him. This time, he turned over, face down into the pool, "Whoa, yo, whoa, what-the, hey man, what's up, what you doing, nah, c'mon man" or something like that or none or that.

Cameras swinging from my neck and banging into each other as I entered the reflecting pool.

Me and the reflection of me, upside down, worrying the surface of reality. Tapped him, pulled at his shoulder. He turned over. His eyes were there. He looked like a version of John Seward Johnson II's The Awakening, the sculpture of a giant struggling to rise from the earth or struggling to free himself from whatever the earth is. For years the sculpture made its home at Hains Point and was a popular local attraction. It's where we (D.C. teens) played hooky, went on dates and hung out after proms. Standing above the man in the pool, I had the feeling that I'd been here before. I did not take a photograph (with the camera) of him looking up at me but I did with my mind.

I needed my cell phone to call for help but it was on the bench. I splashed back. Dress boots and slacks. More splashes. A camera flash in wet daylight. A Park Policeman had arrived, on foot, and was running noisily across the liquid mirror toward the man in the water. He was white. He reached him, began to pull him up. I shot as many frames as I could from the wide pathway and the stone border of the pool. Another cop arrived. More shots. They pulled him out. More shots. Without the proper context, especially today, the images are very misleading. They asked if I would send the images as evidence of what occurred. Yes. A few weeks later I got an email. The man's name was Lee Webster. He was having a stroke. And despite the sun and the offer-ground, he survived the sacred pool of sacrifice.

Neoclassicism for Folks East of the River

1,
1 First Street,
1 First Street, N.E.

Tholos,
      skull cap,
            columns: 24 in the chamber.

      Marble from Alabama,
      Georgia,
      Vermont.

The tourist sees a flagpole that stands
like a native
standing
at a bus stop,
fly ass peristyle.

The native sees privilege,
boiler plate
and belt course
not the Rite in Show Your Right.
The Oven had to go
    as did
  the asylum.

Authority and contemplation in the Age of Domes,
domes in love
with their own
reproductive views,
the meeting place
between symmetrical shapes
and colorful Siamese row houses
                    trained
                        to mimic
and pay-no-mind
the inauthentic replicas of spherical truth
between the building
and the grounds,
North and South extensions,
Indians vs Knights,
a Federal
        Revival
of cast iron violence,
cupola and skirt,
a free energy generating system,
a slow mass extinction,
hoping the road
is definitive.

Cherie "Sweet Cherie" Mitchell, 2009

Paul "Buggy" Edwards and Bobby "Bob" Terry, 2007

151

You the People, you are the prepositions in the grammar of the pocket. You interrupt the sentence with the parole of flavor. You govern the spatial relationships between the drum (subject), the congas (verb), and the cowbell (adjective). Shout out to the agitators among you, the ones who failed in school but who break and beat the rules into their own maps of Washington filled with the grid and grind and life-long road, grooves and rhymes, of patterned freedom, "Where is all that Northwest 'at' Crew 'at' y'all?!"

152

Nothing calcifies the core of crank like not being able to perform outdoors. Stuck in the atmosphere between waters, one ATM facing another ATM like boom boxes reproducing the temperature of percussive weather. To decalcify, crank will need the energy of the heavens, all of the heavens, including the war.

153

At the end of "(Live) Comin' to the Go Go/Simpson's Groove/Charlie Brown)" one of the songs on the 90's *Goin' Hard* LP Chuck says, "Don't drink and drive, you might spill some" and "Excuse me while I disappear, my dear. My dear, excuse me cause I'm out of here. Bye bye bye..." That shit brings the D.C. Bamma in me to tears every damn time, has for years, in every city I've lived; and this morning again, yes, in big moon Missoula, I get misty.

154

If sound matters, sound matters. If money matters, money matters. If the audience matters and it matters to the audience, then who is in the band might also matter. Might not. If the music is not original, nothing matters, not even the money, but if survival matters, you can't have too many other matters, nah, not in a small town.

The conga player sitting, congas on the floor, a Golden Age bamma thang, sun above the National Mall. Then one day, just like the caveman, the conga player stood up and the city, and sound was made modern by that bright moment which we now call the pocket. Some say it began in the up-high, air traffic, air pocket, pocket of air, of urban turbulence. Some say Sir Africanus Conga formed it with his bare hands from sonic clay.

The pocket
has sunrise,
rising in Osiris.
The pocket
has day. The pocket
has sunset,
setting in Set.
The pocket
has night,
guarded by Nut.
Crank, an ankh,
a Sirius Company.
Like the club tore-up
underground,
crank moves
through the
changing sky
of the pocket
then, seeing its own creation,
the hollow rooms in the sphinx, dies.
Horu(s), yes,
your hours
have eyes.

I don't want my life to go national. I don't want the nation to go live with my life, neither "going" is living nor do they have any chance of sustained love, neither is natural. Let me love a local love, locally. Let me call that love home and not by the name of any land or family. Let me be as free of governance as the slowest conga player in the drum circle. Let me fall behind the greedy perfectionists of time, stuck between numerals in a too-hype dance craze. Who and what tours most, the tourist or the sound that becomes a hit? I want to come home to GoGo so much GoGo that I don't even notice that the sign says Welcome to GoGo not Welcome to Washington, D.C.

157

The Grand Order Grand Order of GoGo

If you have legs
and your life ends,
you are a legend.

You are a legend
if your life ends
and your legs last.

158

The only crank that matters is the crank that cures death.

159

If it takes you all of your life to get to the top in your city or you've been on top in your city for more than thirty years then something is wrong with your city.

The GoGo Pocket owns so many people that the people in the pocket think they own the GoGo Pocket. GoGo has been arguing with itself, its own divided soul of rolls, since the sting of the Vistal International Hotel trap. The enemy of percussive opinion is the enemy of percussive people. Sometimes, GoGo tries too hard to be its own God, twice, so hard that its enemy comes from within. Sometimes, after an injury, it has to loan itself an organ or a limb wrapped in the protective gauze of soft reverb.

When Little Benny asked, "Is that what makes you act like that…," he was exposing and celebrating the cray (crazy) side of crank to come, the helluva ride and mental trip between "Body Moves" and "Body Snatchers." Only students of the Pocket Mystery School (PMS) and those who frequently attend Secret Society performance-seances have a true clue as to how the order progressed from "Drop the Bomb" to "I Heard It's the Bomb." Only they know that "Altogether let's boogie" is crank code and call for an alchemical process. And they ain't telling.

The Chuck Brown sound is the most romantic music in GoGo and if you listen to early, live versions of "GoGo Swing/Moody's Mood," the exchanges between Chuck's vocals and John Buchanan's playing is one of the most perfect duets in GoGo History. This type of GoGo love-lock for playing together is usually best expressed between drummers and conga players but can also be heard between Benny Harley and Mark Lawson. "Mer-Sa-Dees," an eargasm. Both pairs of men sound like they loved, not only playing together, but each other.

The purpose of crank is to destroy the cage.

Tyrone "Jungle Boogie" Williams, 2009

GoGo vs Go-Go

TIGHTEN UP BEAT

Youngins'
in a

Bounce
rush.

Old Heads taking time out
and backing it up.

One comes from
the other.

The other
is headed
to the other.

Skating rink,
Crystal. Skaters,

round & round

the
Kollassal
social gap.
Timbale Kings.

165

The Two Red Bars on the Flag of Washington, D.C.

GoGo is not on The One. GoGo is on The One On One. GoGo was on The One until The One On One added another One, an equal one, equal in length and width to the other one, an equation to one-up the law of the Hill.

166

What if music, the pure cultural spirit-offspring of sound, dropped out of the D.C. Public School System on purpose, by divine design, so as not to continue to deliver the youth to a system of indoctrination designed to create a perpetual underclass?

What if it was taken away in a sort of reverse psychology, to make us fight for it and force us to create and glorify an unguided replacement, a not-so-musical non-musical rival posing as a genre so that, ultimately, we'd want the former indoctrination even more?

What if, by protesting to get music back in the schools, we are unknowingly preventing young minds from achieving their highest, higher than music, potential? Sounds absurd but what if entertainers are paid to say, "Stay in school."

167

What is in your heart, the pump me up of it, that it cannot be known or reached into in any mode other than your own broke, style of turning things out? To complain about the arteries of youth is to narrow their avenues, the widening veins that express and decode age differently than yours. What is in their hearts, the bounce of it, that they cannot be accepted or translated into a compatible mode as lucrative as yours once was. They bounce because you pumped them up, and you should roll with it because someone, a soul from the navel of the world, asked them for their young bridges thirteen times.

Glory to the Opposite of Rest

Regarding Rest in Peace (RIP), Power, Pocket, whatever. This is just a Verbal Trick Move, a casting of a spell, as in if enough people say it, the soul that leaves the body has to listen / obey and stay in this realm of material / body kin. We know there's no rest. We know this because the beginning of life and the end of life are the same—just like a row of rototoms, small round, mid-round, larger round.

The e-flat eternity of rest is reset. Boogie is beginning, the breath of dance.

Before you came here, you were not resting and you won't be resting when you leave, even if you get famous and trapped and called back due to your earthly popularity. People who are named after names and who get schools and holidays, etc., named after them never leave this realm. They become buildings, streets, highways, schools, statues, parks, airports, stone. They are used to ground us, to cement reality, to anchor spirit and keep us here.

See the trick, the management of man, the magic. Government is Magi.

A Gospel GoGo band should make a song trumpeting that the opposite of rest is not the work of churchyard burials, alternators disguised as altars, communication tower spires or the obsidian glass of time manipulation.

Consciousness comes into us daily and consciousness leaves us nightly. Consciousness is clearly the God we are all a part of, the God we help have an earthly experience, the God that helps us eventually have an ever-enlarging solar (Soul-er / Sole of your feet / hot feet / beat your feet) experience.

The earth is something of a school—public, private, secret and a test that can't be destroyed. We move through the levels of it in stages; its resources are plentiful. Don't be scared. Scarcity is the way the enemies of nature scare the city. They even lie about the morgue-meaning of cold chillin'. They even lie about the origins of winter.

After years in the pocket, you can't put crank in a box. Fearless crank does not stop once it escapes the box. It cranks in the space between the box and the thing the box is in and so on, encountering many boxes. It does not stay in its lane. It moves from idea to deity, "i" meaning the ego and ego meaning where it's going. Starting from within, the light within, crank builds bodies for our ideas.

170

Artery, Vein

A venue is an avenue where the energy-in-you is stolen.

Like Venus,
it is the Evening Sun
and the son
of Eve.

171

One day, soon, a Lead Talker will realize and accept the responsibility that he or she has the power and support to reach more people than the avenue named after Dr. King and the park named after Malcolm X. This is what all of the people trying to get a hold of GoGo are trying to eliminate, the maturation of an uncontrollable GoGo consciousness, a freer people in the pocket, not just a well driven beat.

172

There should never be more than one tambourine played onstage at a time unless one of the tambourines is played by a right-handed person and the other is played by a left-handed person standing, preferably, at opposite ends of the stage like moons orbiting a full, kick drum or a wheel in the sky pulled over on Kenilworth Avenue by cops who used to be bouncers and wish they were Redskins.

Preamble

We, the People, are the pocket.
We, the pocket, hold the population,
   the posterity of crank.
We, the posterity of crank, are the socket.
We, the socket, provide the energy,
   the energy of spotlights.
We, the spotlights, are the monuments.
We, the monuments, reflect in pools,
   the pools of a perfect union.
We, the pools of a perfect union,
   are the united neighborhoods.
We, the united neighborhoods, are the crews,
   the crews of rebellion.
We, the crews of rebellion, are the public schools.
We, the public schools, are the general welfare,
the general welfare of home rule.
We, the rulers of home, are the Control Board,
We, the Control Board, are the PA System,
   the PA of the Park Service.
We, the Park Service, are the cemeteries.
We, the cemeteries, are the calvary,
   the calvary under the hill of tranquility
We, the hill of tranquility, are all four Congressional congas.
We, the Congressional congas,
   are the former coroners of the city.
We, the city corners, were the beautiful life,
   the reality of black love.

Folks mad at the rototoms for being mad at the pocket for containing slow grooves that you can hold a drink to without spilling it, for being stuck on the ground and allowing all that dying and killing in the District of Crank. The new youngins' haven't lived through this. Many of them hear the pocket, plugged into a socket, and feel no human electricity, no surge. Many, not all.

Bounce Beat is powerful enough to be its own higher-than-sub, sub-genre, because it's more anti-gravity than straight GoGo. Bounce is grown now. Straight GoGo is an employee of the City. Bounce is the Riot and the Revolution, the noise they hate more than heat, a youth inferno. If Bounce does not bounce away from it, Straight GoGo will be used to crush Bounce.

I be seeing the future as it becomes the past, past the present. Whoever, properly, continues the craft of opening the high-hat, also continues the fight against Native Washingtonians re-becoming property. To artfully open the high-hat is to open a portal, a percussive one, and all percussive portals are potentially explosive political. If Bounce Beat adds a Hammond B3 with a Leslie, game over.

175

for Chi Ali

The best lead talkers are lead listeners. What goes in, what they hear, comes out, comes out as them. The best lead listeners are lead followers. Where they go, getting lost on purpose, creates a path, a path for others to find themselves. The best lead followers are actually lead leaders. Their goal is to make the front of the band equal to the back of the band and the back of the band equal to the front of the band. No lead talker, listener, follower, leader worth a damn ever forgot that it is the band that's on the dancefloor and the crowd that's onstage.

Steven Thomas Herrion / "Buggs," 2009

Eaton Nocturnal

Willie Irving Gaston, Jr.
1968-1992

"Slow fast my man passed"
Steven Thomas Herrion

Day is made of math and work but not night,
night is made
of sound and words,
   the Word.
Night has
its own vocabulary.
Night has denser definitions than day.
Day is letters.
Night is numbers.
Algebra is age.
Algebra dictates behavior.

      So many variables,
      The World
      is different
       at night.

There are many spirits in Eaton: eat, at, ton, to, on, no
and not.
Syllables
and beats.
Subtract the E
and it looks like atom,

a tom tom,
the atomic drum's
mic check,
an Adam,
Adam Brown,
the first farmer in the garden,
the first gardener
in the Farms,
a damn project,
a damn paradise
as dangerous as Eden.
No aid for
the Mudflood,
the drum in redrum held up to a mirror
in a funeral home.
  Every Eden
has a grill for ribs
and a Disco Trash Tree
whose fruit
is as forbidden
as the firth sterling steel flight
of an Air Force Base.
All spells,
  all spellings,
     all math,
        all magic is
      as tragic
  as the silver
of sardine skin
glowing in
a bucket of sound

like stars
swimming
in Birney Homework.
Just maintain a grade point average of 2.0.
Who would
sit him
in a seat
with a split in it
then place him
on a throne in the pit
with those who want to weigh-in
with a heavyweight
and reset Southeast?
Only a God that is a verb not a noun
would do that,
one on the rise,
a son of a Gaston
just like Chuck
who was from Gaston,
North Carolina.
In the beginning,
in the end,
was the
      Word
and the Word
 was within Junk.

G

After A the letter G has had more crank enacted upon it than any other letter in the English language. Without the letter G, there would not be a sufficient way to name much of what occurs in Washington, D.C. as well as its ingrown inner bodily function: GoGo. At times, the letter G seems alive and thus deserves a creative and wild exegesis such as what follows.

The letter G was introduced in the Old Latin period as a variant of C to distinguish voiced / g / from voiceless / k /. The letter Y (from the Greek I) is sometimes a vowel. Vowels, the volume of the well, are the weight (in sound) of the water and bodies of water are the vowels of geography.

The wellness of a word, its flow or flowering, is not determined by its meaning but by how many vows /vowels its container (or consonants) can hold, while in operation, silent and aloud, and in what configuration they are arranged. The more vowels in a word, the more structured the word is with the wellness of primary water. Education is one such word that contains all five vowels. It has reached a higher degree than a word with less vowels. Removing the vowels from a word is like removing its nutrients, the entrance to a new tree. In terms of spelling, vowels are the vitamins and the vital minutes of word of mouth. In geography, rivers are the veins that carry vitamins to the land.

An initial like G, on the other hand, is a sign and a symbol that has had its readable vowels removed but not the presence of its phonetic ones. G is the sing and symbol of many things in Washington, D.C. It is both reduction and enlargement, postcard and poster.

The land along the Potomac was chosen because of its geographic versatility, its composition of sweltering consonant and vowel, the spell and swamp of strategic sight. Someone placed a G, the Greek Eye, inside a Y then someone found it. G for government. When the Atlantic Ocean was a window, one George could look through it and see the other George. Their waves were not a war. Their wigs were from the same store. To become a God to the people, the government had to install the narrative of a father among men, soldier and savior, a connective tissue to the crown, and that name had to begin again with a G.

G for Gangsta, big g at the beginning and the little g in the middle. The giant known as Mr. G, baller and picture man. The 24 hour GIANT Food store we hit up after every GoGo, the big G set in brown masonry between brick pillars, the side awnings set in agreeable green to suggest vegetables and the guardians of a garden.

Washington, D.C. is milestone zero for the cult of George, the original first name of the original first gangsta, an OG: The Washington Monument, Busts of George Washington, Lieutenant General George Washington on Horseback, Washington Circle, George Washington Memorial Parkway, Stained Glass Window of George Washington at Prayer, Georgetown, Georgetown University, flip the W to an M and Washington becomes Mason then select the letters you need: George Mason, George Mason University, George Mason Memorial Bridge, George Washington Masonic National Memorial and Prince George's County.

G Count. There are two's g's in George, two g's in GoGo and two g's in Genghis. Ge means earth as in geology or geography, the study of the physical features of the earth and its atmosphere. On the periodic table of elements, Germanium is a chemical element with the symbol Ge and the atomic number 32. [Side note: 32 is the performance name of Dave Ellis, set in post Junk motion by the lack of a 2.0 Grade Point Average.] Genghis also contains "his" as in "his earth." In the word-body geography, Geog precedes Ra and Ra, the Sun God, is Radium. The atomic number of Radium is 88. In GoGo, Rah Rah is one of the performance names of Chris Black. He is also known by Rapper or Rappa Dude. This time, the lead talker, a son of crank, manifest as an app of the sun. Crank does not revolve around him. He revolves around crank.

Earth contains ear, eardrum, the tympanic membrane and the drum of hearing which vibrates in response to sound waves. The alchemical process by which ge became go was one of simple extraction, the vowel or "e-vowel-lution" of evolution, the "e" was simply removed. In time, all vowels will be removed. Yanked from the ground like the central gem of gematria, math, the aria and mother of numbers. Consonants are the shells, more "els," the internal organs of assonance guarded by giants like Genghis Khan. Over time, the event of Genghis becomes George and the consonance of Khan becomes Cohen. King George, a George Washington? Replica or Royal Federalist? Republican or Fed? George Washington in an apron, Gmail or the skin of the lamb? Plaza, a public square, sometimes a Federal site. All rights waived to a few stars and a few stripes. Human flag pole same as the police. Look closely at any badge. Genghis in a flag, a D.C. flag that fit like a coat of arms, the cape of Empire downsized just enough to be a symbol of carrying the city on his back like a turtle. Treason and heroism, it is necessary for one to betray the other on the way to deceiving the people.

The symbolism is worth unpacking. Our city is named after a general not a politician. Our city is a monument-decorated military base. Civilian is a military term. To live here is to do a tour. When you rep the city, you are reppin' the force that comes with being armed. There have been wars fought here, wars against you, not drugs, that's why the drugs were put in you.

George of the Jungle, tribal colonialism mixed with a warning, "watch out for that tree," hanging tree or tree of the garden? Patriotism is just another trapped riot on tap. It and prophecy cannot exist in the same pocket of purpose. The chemist of time turns Valley Forge into Valley Green. Might Prince George's County be the original Ghetto Prince of the DMV? Prince means court, the King's court. King sounds like Geng. Geng sounds like King, the first kingdom of word-made flesh. Follow the kin even when the paint of race, the Giz, attempts to lead you away from the crown of the composition. GeGe is a daughter, the first daughter of GoGo.

A true Prince cannot be flipped by hood status or Statehood or beat into the service of a law or a land that's unfair to the people. Prince is in the blood. Blood is not rinseable. The h in ghetto, heaven or hell, is silent and pleads nothing, not even the 5th. Silence is sound invisibility, visible non sound. It is the thing that all things were separated from. "Let me hear you say, Hell Yeah!" Hell, once meant light and clear or "clear as glass" as Woody Woods likes to say. In GoGo, the spelling of Ghetto remains G-h-e-t-t-o. It did not become Geto as it did in Hip Hop. Scarface with Backyard. Dougie Fresh with Rare Essence, a remix. Salt N Pepa with E.U. Hip Hop is the highest form of hypnosis commissioned to Black Musicians.

Manchuria fell to Genghis Khan and Mongolia Manchuria is the birthplace of the Projects and Project MKUltra. It means Manchurian Knight and is where we get the term Manchurian Candidate. Sursum Corda, a notorious housing project in Northwest D.C, was one of our Manchurias. GoGo is heavily populated with Ballou Knights. Housing Projects or Dwellings are one of the ways that major cities hide and give a false order its mind control and eugenics experiments.

Class is the 2G gadget used to contrive community.

Even the flag of the District, based on the shield from George Washington's family coat of arms, is not what it appears. The piercings in the mullets, which once resembled bullet holes, have been altered to make them look like stars, like stations of the sky clock, like bombs bursting in the fabric of air, celebrity holes not halls. They call it a seal, the Great Seal of the District.of Columbia, but we know to "seal" something means to "lock it" as in to lock us—our pockets into theirs, our ribs becoming bars.

In a Corporate Government, land that has been turned into a corpse, the trick of Statehood is the trick (again) of being the legal property of a crown no matter the Congressional treats. You have to remember that you were here first. You were not shipped here.

It's not GoGo that keeps going. It's George. George. George. George. George. George is Government. The Government keeps going, keeps going in the form of Columbia and George, the C becoming G, the G between the v-shaped legs of the Y. George is both rulers, King President. Military Monarch. George keeps going. George is a Program.

With its ha-ha walls and serpentine gravel walks that separate gardens, George Washington's Mount Vernon backyard overlooks a carefully framed view of the Potomac, rural, romantic and descriptive.

Suttle Thoughts, 2009

Valentino Gordon Jackson, 2011

The Wire Puller

Valentino Gordon Jackson
1956–2019

There's nothing,
not an
amplified thing
either
White Lightening
or the Ether Den of Eden
can do about it,
nothing, the body,
soaring away
from the soul
of the night sun,
can convince
the atmosphere to alter,
no matter
what frequency
or bandwidth
you with,
including
the sky-high garden
of guitars
and giants
in remission
sticking out of dirt,
like bits
and pieces
of the neck

divided into fixed intervals
of life,
the framework
 of the body
—freaky,
 low,
   mid or high,
    an unlimited ointment
      of Virgo voltage
     innacity of
 of monoatomic
   ionosphere,
    the melodic
       quarter clock of GoGo's
       early obsession
            with time,
           with chimes,
         vibration reduced,
         so the cancer
           won't spread,
           like a song,
throughout a pleasant seat
              in the
           pick-less,
      Solo Ether
   like the cure
for physical sickness
  : fluorescence resonance
   energy transfer:
    ion, icon
    or tin ton,
       an innovative antinovel

of a signature lick,
    all the stages
    of being on it
       like Tino,
  made ear-visible
and connected
      to the wire supply in the sky,
  strings pulled
from heaven
and pressed back
    down
  into the
    earth,
     fretting.

Stick Bag Perspective

Think, please, of the first beat of birth: tat tat ta boom or the getting into skins or the getting into heads, the way sticks do, however they became, as virgin consciousness—neither male or female—the sacrificial search for identity forced to depart the divine. Physical thinking not portrayed as drum belly or bubble, not portrayed as the maze-like creases of the brain and not portrayed as the large seed planted at the top of the human plant that wishes to become a tree in the middle of a colony of ideas.

Once we were the trees that grew to and through the heavens. Once we were the breath of fire, the fire spitters, carbon bonfires of speech, capable of the scorching alphabet of the dragon, the twin enemy of the beast, C33 or 6x6. Once our beast-ness contained no art or ark just a spark.

A spark like the chrome between a flame and a fire. Air cells. How one gets an extension—through an atmosphere that is as organic as the weather behind our eyes, the climate we sneeze and the catastrophes caused by a cough—of the self. All mucous is reproductive but it is the mind that alters the material. A daughter in the womb. A son in the world. Through a newborn pours the liquid and stone of passed-on creation, of the age that ends in a mold, the flesh tech, and becomes a slightly changed beginning.

Another non-fictitious take of my personal path.

We were young, no, no such thing, but saw each other before we heard each other, sense not science. Drawn to each other by the hand of premature crank that was sketching us. There certainly wasn't any Rolleiflex in my roll, not yet, no looking down to focus but the entire time the band was setting up, we talked as if standing in front of a tripod waiting for the timer to solidify the matchmaking.

It was Essence and it was in Northwest, up 14th Street, near the Bus Barn at Buchanan, October 1980. Two of them, two of us, all fly. Summer job money clothes. Tootie and Chicken. Itchy and Sayers. We knew the grooves, the songs, had our favorites, could name the band. There was nothing like it. "Railroad Tracks" was hot but more of a first set warm-up vamp and "The Tip Top" was being transformed, slowly, from "Take Time Out" slowly to the end of the soon-to-come "Take Me Out to the GoGo."

I was a good dancer but I was a better listener and an even better watcher. Like Zora Neale Hurston, I carried things extremely well in my memory. Itchy was on the football team at Dunbar. I was on the swimming team. We danced behind the young ladies we had just met, close, but not vulgar. From the stage Little Benny flowed through a simile, "Like Al Capone and Eliot Ness, we gonna hop and rock and do the best…" The young ladies showed the same signs we showed, how could we all see each other again, some other day, some other show? Rhythm makers made by rhythm. And that is what happens to those who live in rhythm, any rhythm, the round hydrogen of matter, of writhing and body writing, especially the rhythm of life and its constant percussive pulse: passion. The passing Sun.

There is a place between beats, not quite a pause, not quite a pocket, but more like a pinch of breathing—a course of entering and the course of knowing, natural knowing, percussive but not rude and, still, not yet a rudiment or pattern or governance of attraction, one thing coming towards another, mind, and another thing coming toward it, body, unregulated except by which that is a gathering of the senses, every limb reclimbed, every tender tendon, fibrous in a vibe. I didn't say dance, no, not yet. A music before it was usable, the most almost-motion ever, but not the flow of the life after life, the light that clots and becomes a liquid or an opening of a door through sound, the silk lining of the threshold into this world not yet a full fall from the mind of the father into the matter of body. A mother, her busy nest, a business.

The blood that carries the fire and war of love.

The water that carries the prison and freedom of language. Their marriage is memory. Membrane. Mucous. Music. The slick dancefloor of the mouth. Their divorce is the violence of voice moving away from mouth, the wonders and possibilities of the physiological act, pre fact. One cymbal hollering at the other. Glued into one talk, the landscape or landing strip of the top of the tongue is a very different texture than the primordial landscape under the tongue. All tongues, like tones, are a tomorrow. Of arrivals and air rivals, lovers. A scheduled spirit visits an unscheduled spirit.

My son, the rise that fell through me, weighed enough at birth to be called Terrell, Fin, and Da Frontline. He stands after Thomas, Sayers, Sticks and TSE. Where we fell has no face, no surface, no two-sided profile of nobility to place upon another and call it genealogy. Every human feature contains a defeat. It looks like one thing, one living thing, then the water moves and it is many other things—not things that were built but things that have grown or fallen into or fallen up from growth. Stone used to grow up from the ground. Sound, too. Same law. It not only looks like you but sounds like the alphabetical biological equator of what beats from within you. Your warmth plus his warmth equals a verbal destiny. The dictionary of life is also a compass. Bloodline, guideline. Map as moment of mothering. Math as the numerical meaning of plasma. All of us standing on a magic square, the ancestor of the numbers game and lotto. Talk like tonk. Walk like spades. I declare the war of reproduction. Dealt cards easy to play but ignorant of the real meaning of the suits. The alma mater of water is plastic matter and the alma water of matter is the mating of the various possibilities of math and sound—the arrival, in orchestrated breathing, of human arithmetic hiding rearranged air.

Nature adds, subtracts, multiplies. Truly, science is no more than an equation of the essence of sight. Elixir. Iris. Sight being just one of the bicameral systems of the sin entrance. All of the senses, known and unknown, are systems of physical and non-physical Assemblies, the lies some have to lie together to see. By way of reason and intuition, crank left the pocket to discover its own cosmic center. To the three-pound brain, the nature of knowing (known) is but an organizing principle set to logic. Philosophy aside: I know my son because when he arrived, one day after

I returned home from High School, his features knew mine. This stage of his rising made extremely familiar to my rising by his complexion and eyebrows, a knowing of me already in his six-month-old unwritten autobiogeography.

No, he hadn't been here before. He wasn't your average returning old soul. His inward look outward was not very common. Me-him. Him-me. The time of eyes, exchanging time. Him-me. Me-him. In another time, let's say in the time of ears, the sculpture of the human head will be slightly different and the eyes won't be allowed to play God. It will be the ears, hearing not sight, that will have the architectural attention of the magnetic currents of love. This is currently the earned privilege of the heart of hearts, the drum. The eternal gaze of the sphinx will be transformed into an eternal listening. Our ears will structure reality and the form of physical being. Aligned, our senses will shift to make room for other senses on a very crowded playing field. The once single player cowbell will take its place on a rack of percussive colored chakras. Some will call it universe. Others will say the human nervous system is a lightning rod of antennae-plasma. The eyes and the ears will trade places and over time all of the senses will become one super sense, rooted, again, in the memory of a one-night stand left standing (and rhyming) among the living for years.

A return to consciousness, one sense, sex only once, just the essence. Science, symbol and the son of sound, left behind. There will only be you, in the love act, knocking at the drum of a door. Which side of the blood-soaked keyhole are you on, which deliverance, which floor? A breathing stillness. Game board and the life on it, 'round and 'round. Walk onto any stage, twist a rototom and return, in time and rhythm, to how all sons are songs. To be drum and sticks, raised slightly solo, in the storm of the self—concert and conscience.

Each of us is given a turn to pattern. We are here to add to one another the parts of the pattern that are removed when we make another one of us. Pattern is parent.

Karis "MsKaris" Hill and Deanna Hawkins, 2011

Keith "Sauce" Robinson, 2007

Reverse Mute Cease Crank Strategy

What if a GoGo Radical Activist came along, let's call him or her Crank X, and said, "We are going to stop dancing and drinking for two months, a self-imposed boycott of all modes of the pocket, a withdrawal from partying, to change our quality of life and create a purer cultural-political base, a leaderless one led by the logic of indigenous individuals?"

Think about it: the dry period of the boycott would affect the liquor industry as well as the political structure that serves and protects the liquor industry. Both would dive into a panic, ultimately meeting the demands of the citizens of the District of Crank.

If you ceased crank for a few months, they would be scared and stuck wondering, "What the hell is GoGo doing and why have Black Folks withdrawn from our trap?" I bullshit you not: they would probably even give every GoGo band ownership of its own Club.

No talking to newspapers, no rumors, no panels. No new releases. No listening to the police they hide in politicians. A solid silence, no crank, for two months with the hopes that GoGo might win on its own terms.

However, being masters of democratic deception, they want you to think the opposite is true. They want you to think they want to and can mute you. The user "they" do not and the used "they" cannot but (together) they will ride a mini drama as an opportunity to land-grab-your-trust, inserting leaders and a victory to hijack your ability to see the true construct and purpose of future conflicts.

Every time you put the U.S. Capitol Building, the Washington Monument, the Jefferson Memorial, the Lincoln Memorial or a flag on your flyer or in your logo, you gentrify (with a capital G) GoGo without even knowing it.

During the early half of the Golden Age of GoGo, the words crank and crankin' were only applied to pockets that were played too fast and whose percussive grammar, the ability to lock a groove, lacked agreement. In those days we watched and read Jungle Boogie like he was Shakespeare. When the Golden Age ended, the definition of crank changed and today crank is a star but it used to be a bum, just banging and bamming-off.

179

Remember when GoGo used to get blamed for violence, the shootings and the murders. Now, being on the payroll of the blamers who work for the enabler, whenever there is an awful crime GoGo will be sent to fix it, police it, and make anti-crime songs about it until finally (thanks to GoGo) there are no more guns in the District except the ones used by the cops and the military which will seem like a good thing because of the shootings of the past—a good thing until the day comes when the citizens and the government finally clash, like an amateur rototom player tired of a microfiche reader, and the people of the city, weaponless, are unable to defend themselves.

180

I can't continue to crank in a conundrum. I am not interested in phones with cameras in them. I am not interested in photographs with phones in them. Pictures and photographs are not the same things. Pictures contain people. Photographs contain ideas. Photo to phono. The fee of self, self-fee, selfie. Right before we sold ourselves, soul-fees, record players used to think and feel for us. The phony no in phonograph was once an on. The easy on was once ho. Now, too, I see rap after the g. A graph that might guide sight. Seeing Aids: Solar Pillar Cult. Hearing Aids: Lunar Pillar Cult. My crank ain't iCrank. No more camera-phone in the phone booth, no phone booth in the pocket. The Socket is not an App. To download an eclipse, you must delete your eye-go and ego and open the aperture.

181

In a white city that used to be black with white citizens that used to be black citizens in white neighborhoods that used to be black with white pockets and white politicians and white schools that used to be black, I heard white crank and met white GoGo.

The 15 Grade GoGo Government (GS) Pay Scale became the CPS (Crank Pay Scale) with less than 3 steps within each grade. And people remembered the black giants of original GoGo with murals and school tours and t-shirts and socket souvenirs and parks named after local legends. And they spoke of the pioneers of the Golden Age of GoGo the way they also once spoke of Negro League Ballplayers.

All of the infinite energy venues were turned into empty shrines and the leftover fossils of the Drummers Breakfast packed away in crates marked crank-a-saurus in the basement of the Smithsonian like museum pieces soon-to-be re-cast in clouds of clashing electromagnetic signatures.

It was all very male-witchy, Mitchcraft, all very Love DC = Go-Go. The madness was finally real. Like a colorful military of Crank Clones, an entire community, onstage and off, obeying the same skin of words under the same spell of alchemical apparel, imprisoned in symbols.

In a white city in a white nation behind white monuments that had all been changed to black and rebranded under the ownership of official, I beheld the zombie-birth of a pale pocket, human souvenirs.

182

Time to admit it: GoGo wiped out and displaced a lot of serious non GoGo groups (who had mature styles) when it captured the bodies and brains of youngins' using them to replace so many talented elders like a generational gentrification. Time to admit it: GoGo was a reset about to be reset again.

183

The why hasn't GoGo gone National question should be banned from interviews, articles and regular conversation, why, because everyone knows that poverty travels at the speed of percussion and percussion travels at the speed of poetry, because just as there is no such place as non-National, there's also no such place as National, because no one other than a poor person wants to party with, sleep-with, marry and raise a family with another poor person. A few poor people are easy to sell or hide in a song, on a CD cover or at a live performance but an entire continuous scene of crank culture is impossible to transform (by outside forces) nor should it be. However, backwards help is on the way. The Pristine Thug Age, which is actually The Pioneer Replacement Program in disguise, has already began to infiltrate and falsely upscale GoGo.

184

The average person indoctrinated by easy American culture is only taught to think critically in terms of competition, winners and losers. I've always believed Crank to be, at its best, a concoction of anti-Conformity and Concrete Noise Expressionism. A rescue mission not an invasion. Everyone who has ever tried to camouflage crank by turning it into figurative shades of green leaves or a garden of uniformed, weaponized foliage, was actually advocating the flag and fashion of terrorism.

185

Every generational beef or misunderstanding between Old Heads and Youngins' can be blamed on one thing: Birthdays and Birthday Bashes. The Battle of the Bands is now the battle of the Birthday Bashes. GoGo was conceived, locally and intimately, in clubs called the GoGos but it was born, nationally and detached, with the release of a studio album. Get rid of the recognition of Birthdays and Birthday Bashes and you will have, at least for a night: peace in the pocket, less cray in the crank, and no bang in the bounce.

There are three stages or prongs on the plug of triflin' but this is not the place to unplug them without snitching on the socket. Triflin' can be translated as talented and if you take the triflin' out of crank, it ain't crank just as if you take the protest out of the pocket, it ain't the pocket. It's not natural to be at the center of every protest in the pocket unless you were put there, put there to control the outcome, to give it a ceiling and to protect the interests of the opposition.

187

What if one type of GoGo, the GoGo that is allowed to leave home, is used to nationally gentrify (or pocket-cleanse) another type of GoGo, the GoGo that isn't allowed to leave home? With so many Men in Black in the Crank, by 2024 it's going to be impossible to separate the aliens from the agents. Hint: the agents are the ones who mix slang with agenda and the aliens are the ones who speak in drum-less tongues.

Quiet as kept, Washington, D.C. and GoGo already has an enormous Crank Cutline Neuralyzer. The red eye at the top of the Washington Monument, the one standing in a vesica piscis like an erect cowbell stick is capable of isolating the electronic impulses in your brain and removing all of your memories, including which quadrant (NW, NE, SW, SE) you used to be from. You won't remember home.

188

The most unstable mental stable, the Establishment, is made up of numerous former radicals who were only radical in order to establish themselves—their Crew, their Quadrant, their Crank, their Legacy—as the New Establishment. Know them by their weak drumming. The right-handed ones can't play cross-handed and the left-handed ones confuse the snares between their legs with their hearts. Neither is dominant and both are dominated by the elected lead talkers of downtown.

189

Symbolique

So many wings in the logos in the GoGos but not enough Slug-go.

190

Saying you created a genre is like saying you created a germ just like saying you make beats is like saying you make bacteria. No one removes the back of a camera looking for its heart but many have removed the front of a bass drum and inserted a brick.

191

Recipe for the Removal of Non-Native Crank Hate

2 twenty-five lb. sacks of congas
stuffed with curry and cumin to
ward off the effects of the scent of
the demographic change.

1 six-pack of TDK cassettes
stirred in the creamy lead talk of
mambo sauce, scribble on the
labels fading like salad lettuce
without a march permit.

10 fatback bass-foots packed in
Vaseline and vinegar, REMO
drumhead stretched across the
top of the jar just to suffocate the
prejudice of turmeric.

8 skinless tambourines, fatbacks
tossed in a yard of rezoned capers
and for good hope a pinch of
eatable stained glass. Can't
complain, though, if the sun of
equality sprinkles race on the rice
and the rice tastes like riot.

Add 3 rare red leaf rototom rims,
pie-shaped *ooga booga* hydrates,
obtained from the National
Arboretum not the United States
Botanic Garden.

Home-cook the crank in a pot of postprandial somnolence oil (it is juice)
and unstructured water. Bring it to a boil but never bring home processed
road *kill at will* on a skillet or a record. If you have to, stop the show not
the protest and wait for the monitors in the minor fights to simmer.

192

What is GoGo without the pocket and its energy source of sockets, a
body without a soul, an egg rising and setting to rest without the spark
of life, the electricity-less shell of an imperfect fertilization, the cell salt
of hi-hats opening in new condos. Imagine (between trips to the bar)
The Moonlite Inn, no, the lit moon in the sky, no, all the light within the
moon without its nightly mask of the map of the Earth reflected back
at us, that (up-high) lunar face you can sometimes see right through (the
parent of all transparency) pretending to present a profile of pores, rock-
cratered, before some hand on the frontline grabs it and shakes it like the
circumference of a tambourine, that which is vacant till the redeemer
succeeds in getting you to remember that GoGo begins, the Universe
did not.

Killa Cal

The skill to kill all ill clowns who think they own
the crown,
Cal,
a Killa,
verbal slaughter in a pillow,
flower bed stealer,
words buried alive,
wake, woke,
riding by alphabets
in a rhyme,
Kill C,
a calvary of grammar artillery,
armed,
all and all
Rare What,
bammas died
Air Cal arrived,
a sin to tax the ground,
a Zilla,
Da Animal,
lick the laughter,
call the killer,
caller on hold, call waiting,
Cal busy
melting haters.
The skill to kill all ill crowns who think they own
the crowd,
stem cell syllables,

lyrical appendectomy,
most dictionary definitions
nose bleed
from his trigger,
Killa City,
Killa Sightseer,
Tour guide
caught doing the Killa.
Killa calories,
la la la,
  la la la.
Cal tolerates
lactose freestyle rants,
reversed.
Spit the milk out
the cereal,
Serial Killer,
Killer calcium for all microphone victims.
Busted lips,
villa rebuilder,
Thrilla bit Manila,
trophies near the ropes,
1st place tropes.
The skill to kill all ill crowds who think they own
the caliber,
an enterprise crowned by success
and natural causes.

194

GoGo has had many original ideas but they were all spoken from the gut
of Crank by the cowbell, congas, rototoms and drums, all at once, like a
protest, leaving all aspects of song and the campaign trail behind.

We arrive via a fall (every time) and love songs express our gratitude to that fall. Grateful and grave-full and still waiting on crank and craynk to go beyond the intoxicating lure of the fall of us that gives rise to love songs, the—seemingly—reverse direction of evil. There haven't been that many, I know, but there is a new horizon, a zone of hours, the rise of Horus, around the statue of Columbia that stands at the top of the U.S. Capitol building, a new horizon full of angels, legends, angels, legends, legislature with bands that you can't trust.

196

When you are "overseas," the people you left at home are also "overseas." Every place with a moving body of water between it and Crank is overseas. Where do you think all that C Natural and E-Flat Debris sank? You do not have to go anywhere to be overseas and you do not have to go anywhere, over ground, to be National. You can't make it out of any place you did not make. Make a place not a name. Names are fake not fate. It's all a matter of the mic check in the mind not the harmful harmony in money.

197

Before they could change GoGo's into Rap Concerts, they had to (slowly) add a two-mic to the internal structure of the GoGo Band and make the new generation all want to be rappers and worshippers of Hip Hop. Celebrity, movies, awards shows and radio were all used to do this. Rap finally owns GoGo. And GoGo helped.

198

Can Gospel GoGo or Christian Crank or Socket Scripture reinvigorate the crusade against "the devil in the pocket" or is it doomed to remain an adjacent or ingrown branch of the Baptist Church, bible-mimcry with a beat?

199

When they walked out of the garden, they took the trees with them. They had no choice. They were the trees and did not have any issues with seeds, no problem with ribs. DNA was and & and was DNA. A for astral not for acid. They are Ras Lidj and Matt Swamp Guinee. Their skin, in some areas, remained bark—yellow, red, brown, black, dark. Duality began in them—one part of their consciousness is in air, the other part in soil. Rooted at both ends. At both ends, a breathing music. A beat it is difficult to beguile. The knowledge of the tree of life, Crank Lukongo. The life of the tree of knowledge, ReggGo. No apocalypse in their pocket. The apples in their throats cannot be eaten.

200

When a peace sign or a peace-i-fix (fresh from a fist) enters the frame, I lower the camera and leave the posers standing there—even if I have nowhere to go, I leave the crab barrel of history and, Strike A Pose struck, head for Alkebulan, "The Land of the Blacks," not Africa, before the club owner, the property owner of modernity, arrives.

Rory "DC" Felton, 2008

Rory's Reeds

Rory DC Felton
1961–2018

No true forests, no flowers or flow,
just the sweet low grass
of dirty burial fuzz
between Railroad Tracks
once lunched on

for rides through the city,
monuments, tuned to perfection,
and passed like joints,
lit as the tip, high as the top,
raggedy hat, unique, but played more than the horn,

roll call rolled like a marble shotgun,
the ammo and smoke of paired proper nouns,
names flying away from memorials
and separated by "uh huhs"
of varying lengths

like an improvised list of vocal life spans,
the do-it-on-down downsize
of inner-city centuries,
the opposite of siced-up fuss,
melodic and vibrato-heavy,

crossing one of those essential bridges
made of brass and breath
& curving, like the end of a solo,

above the river's neglected branch,
gentrified mouthpiece licked
by the bamboo-encased plastic of displacement,

vibrating like a cell phone
in a stenciled anvil case in the back of the white truck
one gets on and off in one of those
vein-like alleys just dying to be an artery,
air blown through

the tubes of Metro tunnels,
inhaled by riders on rails that favor a nasal sound
not stemming from the oral cavity
over the grease-less training of musicians
from Performing Arts Schools

and their access to opportunities
of Higher Education,
Georgetown privileges,
much higher than Highland
or the planned prisons of lost power

we call neighborhoods,
where a green valley, suspicious of high-waters,
Congressional Hearings,
the harm in harmony
and the disharmony in money,

no longer needs the hype in hymns
to prevent the tenor's tide
from rising like a flood of local dying
or the "he say she say" fuss of ROR YE SSEN CE
constantly heard and hushed

throughout public housing
like the slapped faces of opening bands
eclipsed by plastic crescent moon-shaped tambourines
and the cowbell's epic poetry
up-in-the lunacy of club,

the repetitive Hell of headlining shows,
four, five times a week,
a cluster above native energy,
the night that makes local strength
reduced to the realm of invisible worker during the day,

no one downtown able to read the translation
from breathing to sound
your well-soaked reed makes,
nurtured in a glass, near Penny,
one of those sick of your muse nights

sharp as the male knife of sex,
one of those nights when the fruit becomes brown,
the sweet spot that serves the mouth
just enough to flavor another reunion,
one of those desperate nights as compatible

as a leather horn strap,
the dark neck of nothing giving formlessness
to the loss of practical jewelry,
one of those anniversary nights
where there will be
one less legend to mic.

Kimberly "Ms. Kim" Michelle through Rototoms, 2009

The Right Half of *The* GoGo Power Pyramid

The
The Man
The Man said
The Man said we
The Man said we got
The Man said we got to
The Man said we got to go
The Man said we got to GoGo

202

It should not be required of the GoGo pocket to sacrifice years housing the same songs over and over again, night after night just to earn the respect of a local audience. It also shouldn't take a GoGo band ten years, with or without the support of radio, to get the community to feel comfortable with the so-called brand and trust the faces of their sound. GoGo, fortunately and unfortunately, is as personal as it is local and homegrown audiences won't crank with you if they don't know you or haven't lived with you. It's an unreal agreement, a bamma ass contract that has hurt the possibility of many a new direction. Week in and week out, GoGo produces a superhuman amount of crank. In fact, it overextends its craft, exhausting the gears of the gift in exchange for mere crumbs, simply to be liked or heard (as much as possible) at home.

203

"Known to party to dawn," Benny and Shawn are morning stars, sky walkers and workers of the sky. Also ribbons of light and light bringers in the Night Zoo of the zodiac. Their logic, turnt-up, is astrological and when their moods swing it don't mean a thing, it means everything.

204

The Godfather of Sound is Silence

Original music reorders reality. Genre music simply changes the subject of the sound (and the sound of the subject) from one song to another. Songs arrive on a groove, spin, then depart in crank. They used-to soothe before they sang. The soul takes a hit every time one of its offerings is given a number and placed on a chart. To have a hit is to be hit. It's percussive. Sound is the toolbox of Creation, Nature's Creation, no, the creator of nature, as well as where the word cremation comes from: a return to nature, a return to creation and therefore cannot be made by anything except out of a conversation with itself. Every species of song and speech sounds like sound. Genre is only a trendy pair of jeans worn by a generation that shares the same social genes. Music uses humanity, the human instrument, to get back home to sound then shed it and get back home to silence. Silence was first. Every musical instrument you own already exists as an organ within you. Listen to yourself. There's a loud silence in you, louder than anything in the external world but the external world, being a sensory magnet, prevents you from fully hearing you. Silence was first. It is the neighborhood from which all noise grows. This is the last thing that the pocket, the socket and bounce have to learn. The Godfather of Sound is silence. Silence has a sound that can take pain away.

205

After he cranked all winter, Abraham Lincoln entered spring by turning his back to the bodies on the hill in Arlington. He sat in a seat behind marble columns, and waited for his drum-kit, the toms of history that were stolen by memorials and marches, to be returned by the Smithsonian. Every now and then, one of Frederick Douglass's roadies, one who has read Hesiod's *The Ages of Man*, cleans Abe's ear with a giant Government-issued Q-tip. The cleaning sounds like the chatter once heard around the dry fountain outside Union Station where the homeless say, "I don't know how they did it but we are what's authentic. Rome is the replica."

As bad an imported storm as Crack and guns, the use of the N-word helped change the climate of GoGo from mild to a muthafucker. Riding the moods and trends of Rap, it took root in the vocabulary and the behavior creating hard exteriors, false protective umbrellas, that blocked the way to cloudless creativity. Today, even, the attitude that goes with its use is hard to eliminate and can't be resolved by slogans like Cease the Fire or a Peace Ride.

207

for DJ Noise

The images come into the camera with sound, with Crank, and leave the camera with sound. The amount of Crank that is left behind is determined by the viewer's ability to accept the camera as an equal instrument or citizen of the pocket. There is nothing Zen about it. Cameras do not steal souls. They copy the surfaces of the soul's costumes. Eyes are not windows; they are worlds. Photographs look the way they look because of the way they sound. They contain noise. They contain a creation we can see, Crank. Still Photography is only silent to the human sensibility that cannot close its eyes and hear a drum. You don't sell your soul. Your soul sells you.

208

AM-FM

In the mourning
between Outta and Sight
like the sky of his wireless smile,
we can still access
    Mike.

There will never (again) be Golden Age acts with allegorical names like the Soul Searchers, Rare Essence, Experience Unlimited, Trouble Funk, The Peacemakers and Mass Extinction. Built by natural myth (not naturalism or mythology), these group aptronyms each contain some evidence of one of the stages of our journey through this realm and, though hidden in the hard shell of what became urban persona, each provided a luminous instruction toward an understanding of the purpose of our past and future lives as spiritual beings having a physical experience.

Rare Essence

Embodied within this name is the substance of life, the rare survivors of the journey through air, from silence to sound to substance, the wet substance of life wrapped in the light of electricity made flesh, the skin of the outer cement that slowly becomes an inner city, arriving in the hardened vessel of the human form. A rare essence is the time of life before the "head, shoulders, knees and toes" of physical life. In biblical terms it is comparable to Genesis and the time before the Fall, that golden time of the day, that precious metal, one finds in a newborn's hair. Gold means solar essence. One can trace the scent of the perfume to the sun's rays. A young dynamo, the brain is the son of God.

The Soul Searchers

The most powerful ingredients in the spiritual aptronym, The Soul Searchers are the sold sun, the seer and the chair. Look closely, all three are there. Sol which means Sun; Sear is the ear, the listening stage of seeing and three-fifths of the word earth. Earch, being a slight variation of urch, reveals the matrimony of search and church as one of the chief purposes of the Gospel. In biblical terms it is comparable to the Old Testament and our lives within our body, the way a seed begins in darkness and grows toward light to be reborn or planted in consciousness. In the temple of man, the Soul Searchers were explorers and builders of local civilizations and discoverers of the word within.

Experience Unlimited

There's a spear in Experience and where there's a spear, there's a serpent, a side piercing spear, bolt and bite, the crucifix after the E, an eternal crossroads falling into the position and purpose of x. Whatever happened on that hill, on Mt. Calvary also happens in those two words. It expresses a range of the interpretation of free will, of "Do as thou wilt." Some believe a savior died on the crucifix for our sins while others believe the devil stole a piece of the spirit of God from heaven to free the fallen below. It is comparable to the New Testament and our lives after we leave our bodies. Egypt means flesh or anatomy. "Da Butt" is Fleshology, the hidden human time limit built into Unlimited.

Trouble / Trouble Funk

The problem with the Book of Revelation is that it reads as if it has been rearranged, told out of narrative order, and placed in the right place and the wrong place at the same time. It is a beginning and an end, a bookend of a cycle, the original changing same, forced into necessary chapters like Trouble becoming Trouble Funk and Trouble Funk becoming Trouble again. What comes after the revelation is the reset, Creation again, the Eternal Flat Beginning. Reading it at the end is meant to make you think that it is always coming not that it has already happened. Moving it to the beginning proves that birth and death are the exact same thing, "I got the time. Now do you want to funk. Came to boogie down. 'Cause T-R-O U-B-L-E don't mess around." Each book of the bible contains trouble and the truth about the destruction surrounding sound, the bottom of sound. Maybe they did drop the bomb to destroy all earthly conflict.

The Peacemakers

The intervals of sleep between the ages or the stages of man including the return to and departure from the cave, the original cave, the Cave Yard, off to the side in an alley in the silence between dynasties, that unarmed moment between the battles between science and religion, that brief second when they were one and arguing over the meaning of PM and the first noon. And although they lost the war in heaven, their best defense, "round like a ball not square like you out there" is what they sang, leaving the avenue-wide wilderness between North Capitol and Rhode Island, so real time and gun-less seasons with home training could begin.

Mass Extinction

Life is reproductive. It reproduces life and death so they could have been called Mass Evolution or Mass Exodus, both referring to the activities of the world contained in the heart chakra, the geography of anatomy we live in: the body of earth. Earth is heart. Included in the reproductive cycle of life is death, the twin cleansers of Creation, what every birth is—a transference from one world or body to another. We praise the death of our God so why not the death of us because what appears, in nature, as destruction is without a doubt an object of duality and thus, also, an agent of creation. In biblical terms, their horns sounded tuned to ritual and the West bloodline, a mob of spirits sacrificed for its pink substance.

210

There are numerous ways to construct and deconstruct Call & Response and yet we are still stuck in the disguised sameness and bureaucracy of Roll Calls that act alike. We just want our names called but soon the bodies on the list, bored with the hitless list, will jump-list.

Eddie Harris Ross / "Bamzilla," 1977–2011

211

Lines Found in *Cane* (Jean Toomer, 1923) Cut into a Cutline of Prose

Mr. Barry covers the mirror. Eyes left their sockets for the cabin. Each one is a bolt that shoots into a slot, and is locked there. Ned knew, of course. The man leads (Supa) Dan up a black alley, on th wagon, th wagon! Mr. Barry offers Muriel the rose…from his hip-pocket. (Supa) Dan looks at it. Jam some false teeth in his mouth and crank him an youd have God Almighty spit in torrents all around th floor. My buggy was still on the road. Mr. Barry bows.

212

When a person in the pocket dies,
I get an email or a phone call for a photograph.

213

I asked if I could read a poem at Little Benny's funeral. *No.*
I asked if I could read a poem at Chuck's Brown's funeral. *No.*
I asked if I could take photographs at both funerals, *Yes.*

What do funerals
have against poetry.
Nothing.
You can't have funerals
without love.

What does poetry
have against funerals?
Nothing.
You can't have poetry
without loss.

214

In my camera's dark chamber of stagecraft,
the Pocket is analog, Crank is digital and Bounce is virtual.

215

If a lens drops in a GoGo, does it become a rototom? If a rototom drops
in a photographic darkroom, does it become a lens? Playing rototoms is
like using three cameras at once, a trinity of chakras, the spinal integrity
of BassWorx.

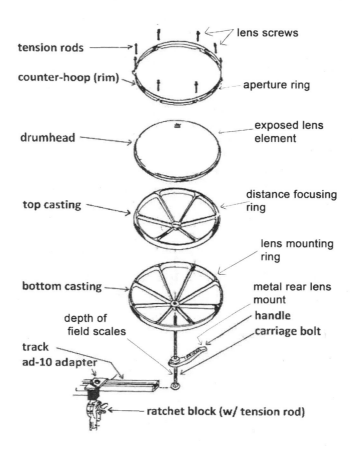

for Carl Jones

CJ's Grandmother's Flowers

Before the Government
dug up
her Eden,
there were
Garden Apartments
made of stone,
living stone,
all over
Southeast.
As long
as there was
a place to park,
no one asked
about the quarry
or the number
 of bricks.
Nothing was
more important than growth,
the moovin'
and groovin'
of young beds
headed uptown
like the bell of a horn
becoming
a sunflower.
The elder love

that results from hands
rooted in dirt,
a crowded show,
two leaves
pulled off of life
and placed on a hat
like wings.
A yard award.
The fertile laughter
of long tones
broken
into loss.

217

In GoGo, longevity is achieved by constantly changing percussionists, by moving them around like chess pieces or mayors but since the social and political game boards of Metropolitan areas are of a one track mind, the control system is always presented as a Youth Movement. Out with the used and in with the ready to be used.

218

Time to, either, stop reppin' places that we only have a surface and residential knowledge of or dive deeper into the knowledge of the place we've been reppin' so as not to be taken advantage of by a past and purpose that was put in place to limit us. Fashion is often a tool of enlistment so pay attention to what you wear. Nothing initiates like Beauty.

219

By accepting injections of Capital, GoGo continues Capitalism. Someone should explain where Capital comes from. Someone, forced back home by Capital, should explain how far it will allow GoGo to go.

220

Now about that candy store that Moe and Joe had; isn't it obvious that candy is code for drugs (?) and isn't it even more obvious that Moe snitched on Joe (?) which is why the song is not called "Run Moe" but it probably should have been. There are two types of "running" in the Nation's Capital, one in Washington and another in D.C. For office and from the cops, a mojo is both.

221

A lot of gentrifying comes from within the community but those leading the charge, attempting to control the GoGo Moment, don't call it that. They call it A Movement. They drop the ment and extract a Moe.

222

When Crank crashed the Party, the pocket became a criminal. P-p-p-p Peedy. Bo Beedy. But when the Party crashed Crank, the pocket, not Crank, became a politician—like the police, an officer, official. Unlike Justice Jay's sturdy lashes, it's not a difference you can easily hear unless you are mentally free so mind your own damn business.

223

For y'all if y'all ain't got no power.

For every child that ever raised an adult. For every adult that ever raised a hand against a child because a hand was raised against them. For every hand that ever raised a stick. For every stick that ever beat a cowbell. For every cowbell that was ever beaten in the pocket. For every pocket that ever beat a block till it bled. For every moved body, crank shaped from all the beatings that ever bled into a sound of the city. For just funnin' at funerals where our eyes may be local but our tears have gone national.

Y'all ain't got no power is a lie.

224

You can put "go" at the end of any word or "go," twice, for more motion, before any name but what does this achieve, the suggestion of opposing forces or the opposite, a site where selection, choice, is interchangeable? All things named are of nature but not all named things are necessarily imbued with the principles of nature or fit for metamorphosis. Go changes, across time, to go. It does not dress different. Its purpose is to trap you in the prayer (the ray) that is trapped in the party (the art).

225

When the calendar calls, GoGo should not respond. It should keep all of its hard ear-earned, slim avenue of revenue in pocket. Stop buying things that cannot create. Crank should not help the calendar break poor folks. Instead of organizing a Movement against someone who asked it to turn the music down, GoGo should mute the holidays, the Gregorian robbers that arrive annually. GoGo should year-flush its own ears.

Stick Bag Perspective

We played first, on the smaller, rickety stage by the entrance at The Moonlite Inn. Every time the door was opened, winter tried to join the band. It was so cold I wore a short, gold bomber jacket (fake fur around the collar), onstage, to start the show and a silver necklace with a small bass drum on it. We wore blue PETWORTH BAND sweatshirts and white pants and, from my end of the stage, I could see both Doc and Darryl Spencer (as well as the others members of Ayre Rayde) as they arrived. Their equipment was set up before ours as if it was their house and that should have sent a message to us as to what kind of night to expect.

Did I show-off, maybe, just a little, spinning my sticks when I didn't have to while the tiny stage shook. We covered "Pass the Peas" which we called "Give it to Nate." Big Nate, our trombone player, was so influenced by Fred Wesley that his young body was already taking on the form of Wesley's.

"Clap Your Hands" was still in its infancy stage but we played it anyway:

> Let's do it, c'mon baby. Clap, clap, clap your hands.
> You can do it, c'mon baby. Clap, clap, clap your hands.
> Get to it, c'mon baby. Clap, clap, clap your hands.
>
> [Break down to the pocket, then sped up clapping]
>
> Rock n Roll Groove baby, c'mon girl, won't you give me chance.
> Rock n Roll Groove baby, c'mon girl, won't you give me chance.
> Rock n Roll Groove baby, c'mon girl, won't you give me chance.

I wrote those lyrics and many of my early narrative poems, bored, in typing class at Dunbar.

We did what we could, out there, near the glow of the Stardust Motel, in the middle of the night in Southern Maryland, far away from the basement in Petworth where we thrived—even then I loved neon lettering and, long before the internet of things, I was into the names of things. Freckled Michael Wade played trumpet. That was a big deal because he missed a lot of shows and a lot of practices and was clearly getting special treatment from our manager, Howard Ross. Being the shortest and the youngest, Lil' Mike was also our version of Little Benny but we never said it or acted like it but it certainly was whispered from the audience whenever we took the stage. His playing was beautiful, his hype man was nice but his lead-talk was too fast. I kept saying, "just talk like you do when you are talking to friends. Use the rhythm of your natural speech. Don't over-perform." Before the invention of the GoGo hype man, skills-wise, he was the GoGo hype man to Kenny Magee (our lead talker at the time) but without Hip Hop as a consistent part of the set, no one noticed.

On the bigger stage at the other end, Ayre Rayde's equipment took up more room than ours, horizontally and vertically, and when they started to play, it sounded like they had a new sound system—like they had graduated from being a little band and had left us behind somewhere in Junior High School with a ton of GoGo homework to do. Their show was impressive, more developed than ours. They were at the beginning of the stage of discovering and utilizing the PA as one of the most important instruments in the band. They sounded like they were not only shadowing but purposely competing with Rare Essence—even their roadies had somehow acquired the poise and uniformity of the RE roadies. While we, Petworth, just wanted to open for RE, they sounded like they wanted to replace RE. I'll never forget that night, especially the way they embarrassed us with equipment power, and the way their lead talker, Ed Winslow, started the show,

"Now Petworth don' cranked, but now it's time to groove!"

Despite all of our Northwest-ness, they were clearly more original at the time and more like the inheritors of the influence of the Total Groove. I simply felt like our band wasn't creative enough and that there was no time to get everyone on the same page before I had to make a decision about whether or not I would go away to college or stay home. We seemed musically-mature only when our keyboardists were playing at the same time as our congas. Fender Rhodes, synthesizer and clavinet. We also had a few lazy positions in our line-up, specifically at drummer and saxophone. We didn't slum that night but an invisible frustration rode back to D.C. with us and when we dropped Mustang, our drummer, off, it was rude and final.

A little more than a year earlier, I had been fired by Reo Edwards from my position with Heavy Connection Band for basically not being experienced enough. In those days, if you couldn't play, folks called you "Sorry." Reo and Robert "Dyke" Reed (of Trouble Funk) sat me down and gave me the bad news one evening after practice at the Club LeBaron. Broke my roto-timbs heart but I understood and made a vow to myself to become a better percussionist in a much cooler band.

A better writer with sticks, someone who could see and hear the whole page of the club, offstage and on. I wanted to play but I also wanted to turn the playing (with writing) into something that named the many mythologies of language that secretly existed between the growing communities and the growing musical form.

I used to ride to (and from) practice with James "Doc" Avery and despite the fact that he was already being groomed to become a member of Trouble Funk (after they were finished using Heavy Connection), when Reo and Dyke fired me, James gave me a great sort of big brother talk about school and music and working hard and making the best of the future opportunities that were sure to come. He was saying goodbye to me. He could tell I was floored and I could tell that he was moving on. Over the summer of 1980, I could feel the patience in his level of professionalism begin to grow thinner and thinner from being in a group with knuckleheads who weren't quite as serious as he was in the same way that he was.

After the firing, I practiced hard, improved a bit, and rejoined Petworth, this time taking my childhood friend, John Cabalou with me. We were better than Heavy Connection, by far, and this time we were on the right side of the management coin. We were our own thing not a farm band for the more established bands to draft from or so I thought. And still, it was jive-frustrating because it was impossible to get band members to sit down and write together. They weren't writers or creative in that way and when we were together, there didn't seem to be time for anything but playing the songs, chanting the hooks, and pretending there was an audience to hear the pretending.

Sometimes, Anthony, our manager's kid brother, would sit on the basement stairs and listen and interact with us. Sometimes a few curious neighborhood girls, who heard us from the alley, were invited in to listen. Their faces were our judges. Their limbs our jury, especially if they danced; it was like a verdict of approval. Of course, we were just kids enjoying ourselves but I wanted more. I wanted to say something. I wanted all of the textures of our particular style, of our percussive vernacular, to become its own alphabet. I wanted it to matter offstage and not just at night. I wanted GoGo to be important in daytime D.C. too, in the libraries, in museums, and in the schools: the ABC's of D Nasty.

Two months after Ayre Rayde spanked us, we opened for Rare Essence at the Howard Theater. I loved the Howard, and being in the Humanities Program at Dunbar High School, I was well aware of the legacy it once held in the upper rooms of the Black Community which included Literature. Minus the marquee with the name of a Greek God on it, the Howard was our Apollo but by the time it got to GoGo and GoGo got to it, it had been in need of major repairs and shut down for years. I grew up on 7th and O Streets N.W. The Howard is on 7th and T, a mere six blocks away.

Having read Jean Toomer's *Cane* in High School, I was curious about the inside of the Howard but at night, filled with band members, roadies, crews, hustlers, playas, honeys, musicians, managers, promoters, picture men, and security, its poverty was well hidden and the theater was nearly majestic to those of us who were new to the nightlife of live music.

In the "Theater" section of *Cane*, Toomer describes the folk vibe of the neighborhood—

> Life of nigger alleys, of pool rooms and restaurants
> and near-beer saloons soaks into the walls of Howard
> Theater and sets them throbbing jazz songs.

Much of Toomer's observation was still there, in the walls, ready to be reworked by the time we opened for Rare Essence. More than 69 years before RE released *Work the Walls* (in 1992) using "Niggaz," the Gangsta Rap version of the N-word as a song title, Toomer used the N-word (in *Cane*) at least 60 times. Some scholar, diggin' in the crate of community in search of an Afrofuturistc nugget, will come along and say Sheraina plus Tomeka equals Karintha. He or she will say this (and acquire campus-cred for it) having never had to turn an open cowbell into a closed urn with nothing but a wooden stick.

We had improved since we played The Moonlite Inn with Ayre Rayde but the sound a half-filled Howard gives back to an opening band versus the full sound it affords the headliner are worlds apart. I enjoyed the three or four Petworth-Rare Essence bills I played on. Had the Miracles played "Going to a Go-Go" there in the mid 1960s and cast a spell that lingered? There was no hiding place in the Howard. My babymuva found me there a few times, half-safe onstage, but when the lights came on, out of hundreds in the crowd, I could see her, only her, seeing me. You were either on it or slumming. I may have played too fast a few times but I never stumbled across or took the bridge apart like I did at the Club LeBaron, not at the Howard. At the Howard among giants, I was an energetic ant in a crumbling legend, a Sayers, not yet a Seer, lifting and lowering sticks like words above a drum.

Ivan Floyd Goff, 2011

The Eye of E.U.

Ivan Floyd Goff
1964–2016

And all those years,
 lookers and listeners,
hustlers and honeys,
  crews and venues,
where was your attention,
on the dance floor, the posters,
the rivalries, getting your name called,
the outfits you purchased
with Summer Job money,
Fly Betty and GQ Rob
looking away from Mr G's lens,
  all those posed years
who did you identify-with,
want to be like, ever sleep-with,
did someone in the sound
make the sound more attractive,
the musicians sitting
or the musicians standing,
Radar, the GPS roadie,
the promoter's fine ass daughter,
  did Bear's big mouth,
always hollering into
the unanswered doorbell
of the microphone,
travel your spine to beltway,
was the map of the District

on the turtle's back
of the conga player's palms
your first rear end tattoo,
where was your attention,
on miraculous limb-rhythmic JuJu,
electric Tino, Shorty Roto-Tim,
smooth Junie, sliding across
    Arsenio's stage,
in a tux, both faces showing,
pocket-loose Fox,
the chance of his swinging arms
swinging your way,
the hard-stepping
muscular puzzle of bones
known as GoGo Mike,
where was your attention,
Ooh la la Tony gone,
    the tall horns gone,
where was your attention,
in the Yard, which Yard, in the water,
jammed in dope,
too working with it, the wetness
to notice the mild vision
    on the keyboards,
too hype to appreciate
the spinal chord progressions,
too "Camay all-over"
to have caught-a-contact,
an ear contact,
with the eye of E.U.,
all of the elements of the hybrid discipline,
the full roll of the joint unrolling

in a Goff Engineered swirl,
if so, then you missed Ivan,
our own Moscow on the Potomac,
where was your attention,
   magic how folks
can dance to you
and not know you exist,
how difficult it is to name E.U.'s lane,
where was your attention,
no they were not the pioneers
the Soul Searchers were,
never an inner-city church
   like Rare Essence,
nor were they, not even in times
of being Buck Wild,
a mushroom cloud bomb like Trouble.
Experience Unlimited
may have been an enigma
but E.U. was a storm
and "Ivan," meaning Gift of God,
was the pre precipitation
   at the center.
Where was your attention,
in the tension between
gatherings becoming practices,
practices patterns,
patterns grooves,
grooves songs,
songs shows,
shows battles,
battles beefs,
beefs funerals,

funerals concerts,
concerts recordings
recordings PA Tapes,
PA Tapes CDs,
CDs money,
money dramas,
dramas breakups,
breakups new bands,
new bands rivals,
rivals reunions,
where were you,
where was your attention,
were you in attendance
when the British Globetrotters
invaded GoGo Live,
"I like booty, hey booty,"
where was your attention,
your subject-verb agreement,
China Boogie shaking
like a white girl in a Colored Cabbage Patch,
serpent tongue to sax.
Go back. And listen-look.
  GoGo back.
     Go off.
And look-listen. Go back
to the daze of butts,
wasn't his fault. He was loyal
and he enjoyed it,
the whole initiation of it,
sticks like bones,
a beat across skulls.
"Goin' Hard" in the Jungle

near the tree of humble,
soft spoken and supportive
but where, what y'all say,
was your attention,
in the tide of Tidy's trumpet
or stimulated by Kent's fingering,
keyboard congas, keyboard clitoris,
if you weren't in attendance,
aw shucks, you missed it,
Ivan, the least flamboyant,
the least "Do what thou wilt"
of the unlimited experience,
nothing like the Terrible,
the least Thelema.
Go back. And look-listen.
   GoGo back.
      Go off.
And listen-look. Go back
and frisk the recorded limbs
of "I Confess," every meeting place,
lay hands on what he played,
because
   "he played
     whatever he could
      get his
   hands on."
Go back. And look-listen.
   GoGo back.
      Go off.
And listen-look. Go back
to the tracks, the national spotlight,
the Big City Groove,

I-V-A-N, "talkin' 'bout Ivan y'all,"
the roll call waiting
outside his house like a radio edit
like Redds ready to bully him
into becoming
one of The Boys.
Go back. And look-listen.
   GoGo back.
and listen-look. Go back.
Dig through the pre meme era of memory,
past cassettes in shoes boxes,
urns under beds,
record cover photos,
the soft focus of looking up into the lens,
perfectly manicured guys,
so goddamn grown and sexy
they almost look gay,
watching God, in the blue and yellow
of studio sky and sun,
the record cover making a cage of sound
and sound making a cage of time,
the whole hopeful group
in a gaze from Tour Heaven,
posed as a studio posse,
politely possessed
and framed in the quick-ending popularity
of yet another Freeze.
Like Kevin "K.C." Muhammad said
when he called to make sure
I didn't miss Big Moe's funeral,
"I'm just gonna stay here and die a musician!!!"
Another graveyard smash.

Must all Ivans, including the ones
without a told story
(or a Tolstoy) end like Ilyich?
Is "Um bop bop"
the only trio
capable of translating
Tsar to Star?
Goff, a godly person,
so much worry-in-the-heart,
the heart of the worry,
even in attendance, paying attention,
lost in the sea of commerce,
we could not hear
or see his name reversed
in the mission
of the navi-gator.
The supreme supervision of a Stephenson.
Go back. And look-listen.
  Go off
    GoGo back
to Ivan, to Ivan,
the eye of EU,
resting like a pupil
and rising like an iris
in The Age of Retinas.
So many high points.

Gregory "Sugar Bear" Elliot, 2008

These youngins' don't know music. These youngins' just making noise. These youngins' don't respect the legends" is all I hear from elders who don't know these youngins' but the Go-Go frontline is what it is today in part because of Hip Hop, because of Hip Hop drama, marketing, posturing and male-movement, because no one brags in unison, in a straight line or while doing the steps of a dance routine. GoGo waves its feet and no one, except the drummer, removing stapled cymbals from the sky, should ever wave his or her arms like an octopus with more than one mic.

It was August, not even midday yet. I was in the shower in a small apartment in Southeast directly across the street from Anacostia High School. All summer the heat was unnatural, microwaves with solar wades. Aftershock, an attack, as explosion in an underground tunnel, Deep State versus Surface State, earthquake is the wrong medical term for the ailment that results from not enough drumming on the earth. To the soles the ground is a grandparent thus while walking through neighborhoods without a real idea where we were going or what we'd find, our feet used to tell us the thump of the tremor and which blocks were hot with the fault lines of buried epochs and cops.

Being alphabetical (alchemical) constructs of language, all chants have dual purposes and meanings, intended and hidden. By asking audiences where they are from (and getting a collective mixed response), lead talkers have explored, without knowing, the hold that the masonic compass and the square have on the city, its residents and grid. Chants also cast spells especially when combined with the ritualistic effects of dance, alcoholic influence, desire or other substances. These chants move the crowd and make em' bounce but once they spread into spells, they become propaganda inside and outside the pocket.

GoGo was not put in place, as they say, "to go national' or to be a free and vital artistic expression. It was, either, designed as a local experiment to influence and control youth culture or was hijacked, by hidden hands, when the Soul Searchers were on tour (1979–1980). It is currently in the final phase of the experiment having nearly eliminated the influence of its elders and delivered the entire genre into the financial hands of the city-state as The Official Music of the District of Columbia. This could not have been accomplished without help from within the interior of the GoGo Community. Just as many of the helping hands that present their handouts to GoGo are anything but helping hands, many of the opportunities arriving in the costume of good intentions are actually harmful steps backwards. GoGo contains a linguistic reset and is being used to reset D.C.

230

Bammas Are Native

"Only bamma in the house, fellas, is James Funk here and I don't appreciate y'all taking my place.

James Funk, Dumfries Skate, Virginia, 1986

Non-bammas
were once slaves
while bammas have always
      been free,
sovereign and loud,

loud in dress,
loud in speech
and against the normalcy of trend.
The Bamma Hour.

You can't control a Bamma.
Bammas go off-script,
off plantation.
They escape Statehood
and hood-states.

They travel and change the places
that welcome them.

Many bammas
have no solid past
        and many have
                multiple origins.

The colors
they wear are meant
to drive the evil spirits
of conformity away.

                A mature bamma
    is like a mystery,
part myth, part street.

    Another
    connotation
    for bamma is off brand.
    Bammas repel
    the Corporatocracy
    and hate playing the role of payroll corpse.
    Want to get off grid,
    kick it
     with a bamma.
     A corny being.

231

Magnitude 5.8

Rippling out from the ground source as if it grew up from the ear of earth, the hearing earth, like a leaf of plant imitating limb and lobe, like an electrical hotspot on a pond on a swamp or an oval pool of reflexes below architectural cartilage, the thick marble shell of skull cap made capitol, whose purpose is to provide a congressional and agricultural rebirth, a bath for the hard, white foreskin of the Republic, all the way from the mining town of Mineral, Virginia, excavated zinc and gold quaking to become crank.

232

Every instrument, internal and external, to the human body is essentially a singer and every singer is, first and foremost, an instrument of vocal expression not merely a servant to words, lyrics and the contemporary structure of song. The toolbox within the human voice cannot be limited to recognizable meanings and sounds. GoGo, not Crank, has been slow to come to this awareness, the awareness that it must explore the strange and become a stranger.

233

Draw a Y
in the center
of a square sheet of paper
then rip the paper, tearing off everything to the left of the Y.
What remains is a spine, the original shape of Crank.

234

Sent away to acquire necessary distance from the reach of the pocket only to be sent back into the depths of the pocket, camera-ready, to properly extract a philosophy of crank from the people in the pocket.

Halima Peru and the Boxer, 2008

There is no equivalent
of a photographic negative
  of sunshine.

The light will burn through the curtain of the rangefinder, scorching the negative or in the case of digital photography, leave a permanent solar stain on the censor.

NEG is Northeast Groovers. The reversal of NEG is GEN. GEN is short for generation. The prefix "gen" means birthplace. The suffix "gen" means produced by or that which produces. A genre is a merger of the renegades of a generation, of the etymology of Sam losing its a and evolving toward Smoke. The best generations produce regenerated sheets of contact, crank repo reproduction, straight from the sky.

If the camera and the flash do not sync (or lock), the reality of the motion of light and the reality of the motion of the moving objects being photographed will be captured by the camera and rendered to the human eye as streaks of spirit and lightening. Imagine the sonogram of Khari's strings, the sound writing of its coiled and plucked vertebrae, the moment, at water, it breaks in a stomp.

There is no equivalent
of a juicy photographic
flash.

Once you realize that the Most Hi (Fi) used sound to create us, you also realize that we belong to sound. It does not belong to us. Humans are tuned. I have never heard an original tune just the germs of genre broken into regional styles. I've heard stereo, the solid-state imitator of Ear Earth, a rebellion against silence, light becoming lyrics, spinning the same form.

237

Once you sell your slave, sound, you can't control what stage, plantation, it appears on. It's not the body of the slave, the people, that was purchased, it's the spirit, the crank, that was purchased and the spirit can enter or be called into other bodies. Sol means sun. Sold spirits don't crank-discriminate. They repopulate the pocket, National Pockets, leaving some folks, locked-in local folks, behind the moon's phase of bars.

238

The closed high hat believes dreaming happens inside the head. The open high hat believes dreaming happens outside the head. When not being night-tapped by sticks, when neither awake or asleep, both types of hat, cocked or turned to the back, prevent the traveler from returning to source and snitching on the collective heartbeat.

239

for Harvey Mason

"Mister Magic" is a light socket and socket of light, the Solomon's Temple, an allegory of the body building a beat, human organism and empire of the heart, the sun and moon, blueprint and cornerstone, the ring and apron, compass and square, the initiate and master, lodge and lion's paw, the degree and secrecy, a great work of consciousness, builder of civilizations and geometric metronome all in a mason jar.

240

To never achieve a consistent locked socket only a locked pocket, the difference being where you place the noteworthy foot—either in both pockets or in both socks, the lower regions of the anatomy (the souls of feet) versus the middle region of the anatomy (the motion of hips). Age as factor, factor as factory, because the stage is governed by a tempo of style that ages faster than taste.

241

for Curtis DK Thomas

Building Ministry

Of the miracles not the radicals around the rim of the word, of the Word, the Word that gave its l and el, its life, its light, to become the world. Of the human library, of the books, ordered into a coded ordering, the purposeful mistranslations. Of the deception, full of cement and bricks. Of "entering" not eating from the tree of knowledge, of thought not thou, of the bark of armor of the righteous, of leaves like pages, of the ages of an eternal text of evidence, of come and see, of common sense as the place of flesh made in the trunk, of the branches of the gospel that grow from groves and grooves, groomed by the stumps of portal in the hollow ground. Of the up and down of architectural horticulture, planted, higher and wider than a skyline of symbols, steeples and temples, written from right to left. Of crank that knows the earth, north, was heaven and heaven, south, was the earth, both being inside of God. Of not waiting for the entire garden of eviction notices to uproot you from the grip of scripture like a make-believe tambourine, a rod ascending into the body of a ring, thrown onto throne, the throne of thinking, not a manger or a cross. Of the prayed-up preyed upon fallen couple, of the idolatry of ethnicity, of the swine of pigmentation, the race from paradise. Of the trick of oxygen not being the breath of God but a knock-off and an appetite increaser. Of the sun that does not show up till Day 4 and the pure light that preceded it. Of the rescinding mist that reveals the revelation of a moment of mystery not mysticism, behold—

> The way
> a Prison Farm
> becomes a workhouse,
> a Workhouse
> begets
> a reformatory,

a Reformatory becomes
a correctional complex,
a Correctional
Complex
begets a garden

a Garden
becomes a park,
  a Park
   begets
   a rec,
a Rec begets
a skating rink,
a Skating Rink
becomes
a bowling alley,
a Bowling Alley
becomes
a lounge,
a Lounge
begets a room,
  a Room

becomes an inn,
 an Inn
  begets
   a hall,
    a Hall
begets
 a hole,

a Hole
becomes a club,

a Club
becomes
a manor,
  a Manor
begets a boat ride,
a Boat Ride

becomes
a theater,
a Theater
begets a temple,
a Temple
  becomes
  an armory,
an Armory

begets a mall, a Mall
  becomes
a community,
a mega community
 of hope,
a Mega Community of Hope
begets a stadium,
    a Stadium
becomes
a coliseum,
a Coliseum,
     begets
  a tabernacle,
a Tabernacle
  a church,
  a Church,
   a house,
    a House,
     a stone.

The Reverend Sidney Speaks, 2007

There has yet to be a full-blown Conscious Movement in GoGo, a crank that balances (and even repairs) the urban musical rift between the pleasures of the mind and the pleasures of the body, a smart party as intellectually stimulating as it is full of the vocabulary of physical attraction. Body, take the mind with you when you Go. Mind, don't leave the body behind you when you Go. One Go without the other Go is half of wholeness, half a tongue, half an idea, half a GoGo, a GoGo without a dancefloor, a dancefloor of substance, a dancefloor without anyone on it that "knows" how to dance. Knowing how to dance is knowing how to think, physically. Knowing how to think is knowing how to dance, mentally. Once Go and Go are in a balanced exchange, an activism (or awareness) rooted in substance, the substance of syncretism, will permeate the crank with the awareness to beware of Movements minus balanced mental motors.

Expressed as a double spiral, a spell of repetitive spelling, like a well-balanced structure of twin, curved pillars, GoGo will always be split and good at hiding its diminished middle. Once there was a third pillar. One side of it will always disagree and stand in opposition to the other side even as one pretends to follow the other in the strength of structural solidarity.

The split, akin to the anatomy of one side of the human body river no longer matching the other, was built-in to make D.C., its crank center, functioning as a lowercase Capital, a corporate entity, a corpse ready for autopsy, and a whole in reality divided by dying but what if there was a flipside, not a flagpole, a way to make the G's in GoGo face each other, and freak each other, time colliding from both sides of the timeline, free till they function as what looks like one neutral o, already naturally noisy.

Faceless, they still manage to long-o-face you like the wheels of a car rolling away from itself yet leaving enough of itself behind to survive. Without the split, the severed sound, the city would fall.

Capitonym

To make
the connection
between "sice"
  and Sicily
  or Sicilians, the Dark Italians,
and siced civilians,
one must give
  the proper nod
 to the proper Don: darkness
or the figure
    in the shadows,
the figure on the hill,
the producer.
Washington, Diocese.
So many Catholic Schools
  in the District,
the District must be
    the military
        holy ghost
of the Caesar's Empire,
Vatican City, D.C.
Vito Corleone
  & Shorty
    Corleone.
The Godfather,
The GoGo Godson,
God the Father.

A pocketful of Mafioso Priests
 capable of hiding
 Gregorius
in Gregory,
Sugar in Saint
& a spina in a circus, a circle.
Spina, Minnesota.
Snakeface Boniface.
To make
the connection between Latin
and the Los Latinos.
Pops, Pap,
Papa, Papal, Pope.
John Russell Pope.
La cosa nostra, La GoGo Nostra,
our thing.
Like an army,
like a soldier's covenant,
glowing salvations were not
the only business
        the Ciceros were about.
The Rosicrucian Rose
     of silence.
  A crucifix in a paw.
A Pope like Curtis,
 like Pops,
   who can move the sun
to midnight,
midnight to Rome
and Rome
  to an enclave
along the Potomac.
America has thirteen cities named Rome.

Underboss Swagger.
Chuck Brown is crown.
Note the rings,
like jewels,
on the album cover.
To mend the stormy moods
between
Medieval
& Mediterranean
releases,
cover them
with a tender,
formal act of submission,
with an Odyssey
of 2001
ring finger
kisses.

245

If it's still a song, it's not original. Original means all origin. All origin means Genesis, the place of beginning, the origin or mode of formation of something. The enemy of formation is formula. Industry nurtures formula. Song is sound prison. Formula, like Science, hides the song in a pattern, an equation that imitates either Destruction or Creation (D.C.), a choice of formats, a creativity you cannot hear until true origin, the twice-inverted OG, the Original Genesis of GoGo, unearths it. Radio fell, like a star, from the word radiation. A hit is in no way an indication of originality, especially a hyphenated one. No bridge in the go or the going, just go. Once a star hits the ground, it either becomes a rat or a rock as shiny as aluminum. The alum of formula is fame. Theme song: "I'm gonna live forever." You might live forever if the right label buries you on a chart. A short-lived flame. There it is, on the face of Gnosticism, the Complete Songs of GoGo Nostradamus, a box-set, wearing a mask.

246

The Solar Cycle of a Groove

Many believe that, like a needle on a record, the sun and the moon both travel above us rotating (at different speeds) in the key of life. One a 45, the other a 33 1/3, widening and narrowing in their spiral paths and beginning again. In their lanes, they stay. Ever stand near the stage and feel the groove rise then set or does it move toward you then away from you? Moving above our plane, as tides become time, sound is planetary. Gravity begins where the groove ends, the groove ends when the grave contains just enough weight to ground the vital organs of hatched orbits. The pocket is like a cosmic egg—flat, spherical and hollow. If the stage is mature, all three realities can occupy it at the same time before either has to re-up, re-down or re-around just like those days the sun and the moon are in the sky at the same time, daze we think nothing of. The solar cycle lasts the entire show, the full evolution and metal age between meteor and metro, all the pieces of the firmament shower, an all-star blend.

You can't run from the crank because the word ran, the past tense of run, is a majority shareholder of Crank Stock. When you invest in crank, you are investing in legs, in the outcome of one leg replacing the other leg throughout the human energy field. On the physical plane, crank is the chaser not the chased. Those who run from the crank lower the market value of their etheric bodies and become babes under the temple bar.

247

Just like the pocket before it, crank can make up for mediocre lyrics, but it cannot replace a lack of drive. There is no such gear as Gentle Crank. Crank is not the software of life. It will not search out Chromosome 8 or standardize you. The intention of the cowbell (in groove mode) is just as focused as the cowbell in crank mode. It is self-updating, and with or without self-care or self-respect, crank self-resets, beating the beater.

248

Metro World

The brick walls left standing like a pair or Matadors:
A mansion that burned, Byrne Manor.

249

Nowhere original to go, caged in category, the original nowhere to go.

250

You out there, the community audience, the citizens of crank and the people in the pocket, are equally responsible for the continued miracle of GoGo because when GoGo began, soul-ing and searching, you accepted the call to the floor. Some nights you entered the pocket with a perm and left with a bush. Other times you entered with a bush and left with a heavy sponge of water. You did not need a seat, Senate or House, to be recognized or heard, or to fill the room—Panorama, Maverick or Squad—with moves. All you needed was the voltage of our most lasting vote: us!

The Audition

1986

Some years earlier, 1981, when I heard that David Green had been suspended, I approached Miss Mack about backing him up on rototoms and timbales but she told me—point-blank—at the door of WUST Radio Music Hall, that they already had a backup named Alonzo, so in 1986 when John Cabalou put a bug in my ear that RE was looking for a replacement again, and asked me to roll with him to Breezes Metro Club, I didn't get too excited. I had been out of the game a few years, studying in Alabama and at American University in D.C. trying to ignore the aspects of the streets that had created me.

Having grown up on the individually distinct style of Benny Harley and James Funk, I did not particularly like the two-in-one lead talk approach that RE was trying out with Cabalou but he was "my boy" so I was supportive. When I left GoGo for college, Cab and Petworth moved on without me, growing in ways that made me wonder what they would have sounded like had I continued to influence them. The slick "4, 5, 6 got to give it to Sticks. 6, 7, 9 just-a keep-a whatcha doing Skin Tight" that I wrote had been reduced to just Skin Tight's part. At first it bothered me, but I got over it.

There was a decent crowd at the Metro Club when we arrived so although nothing was planned, I got a little show-buzz just from the vibe. RE was very particular about style and look, so even when you did not know they were checking you out, they were checking you out particularly the way you carried yourself and whether or not you could attract an audience that attracted more audience. I won't say who but during the three-week period of my audition process, someone high-up in the organization said to me, "The band members attract the ladies and the ladies attract the hustlers and the hustlers attract more ladies and those ladies attract more fellas." I hadn't thought about the social aspects of the RE business model but they had always been and were great at implementing the balance between talent and tease. Aside from Cabalou, my friends in the band were Donnell Floyd, GoGo Mickey and Derek Paige, mostly due to the fact that we had all come up in GoGo during the same period. It wasn't long into the first set that Footz gave Cabalou the nod to invite me onstage. I did not expect it but I was thrilled as I slid next to Mickey near the congas and timbales and was handed a cowbell. With Mickey on one side of me and Footz on the other, I thought I'd try something different. I'd heard David and DC play the bell numerous times over the years so instead of proving I could imitate the classic RE sound, I decided to combine the styles of DC and David into one cowbell sound. Go back and listen to the RE Riggs Bowling Avenue 1979 recording and listen to the warm up to "Body Moves" with the cowbell continuously coming through the echoplex. The sound is multi-bell. That night I played in the pocket a few times then left the stage. It felt good. Footz shook his head, that smile, in what I felt like was approval. A few days later when I was setting up a practice with Mickey, he said that Footz told him that he had never heard the cowbell played like that which I was shocked to hear because I had simply combined styles and pushed it through the echoplex in my mind.

The next weekend I went with Cab to another show. This time somewhere up Pennsylvania Avenue, the southeast side, past where Morton's used to be, top of the hill. I think it was in a Catholic Church. Cowbell again, this time on "Shake It Don't Break It" and a few other songs. It was too easy, so easy I may have gotten too comfortable and got it wrong. At this point "Do it on Down" and "The Roll Call" were still in the repertoire, so there was a lot of classic cowbell work to cover. Mickey said it best, "What you think you hear is not always what is being played." If the cowbell is off on either of those songs, it's glaring. On the later the bell has to hustle to keep pace. On the former, it leads.

Up next, the very next night, Cheriy's. No one invited me, but the band members who were trying to help me get in were also trying to get the members of the band who did not know me comfortable with seeing and hearing me. This is an old strategy and not necessarily a sure one because if any of the people who are trying to get you in are in conflict with the founders or the foundation of the band, the whole thing could backfire. I don't remember much about the show at Cheriy's. I remember being onstage with the band, some cowbell, but mostly listening and continuing to familiarize myself with the current repertoire, so that by the time the official audition rolled around, I had as much under my belt as possible. Even if I sort of felt like an outsider and an apprentice, I soaked up those shows but the closer the audition got, the more anxious I became. Cabalou was fading. He didn't seem to have a real friend in the band. He spoke highly of Footz and Mickey but the presence and influence of James Funk could still be felt as he was still around physically. "I don't know how much longer I am going to be in the band," he would say, "Something's not right." The RE lead mic had to be an internal one, manned by someone who could truly control the band onstage. It would take years for Cab to acquire that. He knew that, at best, he would be either driving someone else's car or sitting in the driver's seat of a car that was being driven from the rear. In fact, that's what it looked like and sounded like to me. And still, deep inside, I was disappointed. He was at the top. This was it. The reason we listened to all of those tapes, the reason we joined those other bands—to get better, to be recognized as being good and to play with the best. I couldn't tell if he was scared or if he felt that the RE he had joined was no longer the RE that raised us and that we both loved. It was hard to tell, but sometimes in our conversations he gave the impression that, although it looked like he had joined the band, he was still auditioning.

My favorite show of my audition process was an outdoor show on a warm early evening at Peter Bug off of Potomac Avenue in the part of Southeast that people who were not from D.C., were not afraid to visit. This area was loved because it was within walking distance of Capitol Hill but not Capitol Hill proper and because it was not across the river.

Pre-gentrification, Peter Bug still had the hue of a village. The energy of the people who came out to see RE when they played outdoors for free was like a physical anthology of inner-city tribes, first generational GoGoers, newcomers, including members of upcoming bands, the whole neighborhood, young and old. I ran into some of the people I knew when I was heavy on the scene, "Where you been Sayers, you with Essence?" Best to chill behind the speakers to avoid explaining, "Nah, I'm just hanging out till the audition," I told a few people. The silent treatment was still in effect, wise not to get too close to the guy who might not make the cut. At Peter Bug, I finally got to use the sticks on the timbales but just the occasional hit, accents, here and there, so as not to overdo it. Mickey did his best to include me, but there wasn't a whole lot he could do since I wasn't officially in the band. Without a doubt a few of the big three were keeping an eye on me, while I believe Floyd, DP and Mickey were carefully looking out for me. I was most comfortable reaching out to Mickey. Later during the week, I went to his house and we worked out together on rototoms and timbales, practicing the RE percussion catalog. I could do it all (as well as solo) but, again, being able to play it alone is not the same as being able to play it with the band, especially one that was used to hearing it played by the originator. No excuses. I would have gotten better but I was not as good as David at being David and it wasn't clear (at that point) what they were looking for. At the three shows, I had not been asked to roll across the bridge, back it up (roll) or play the riff-exchanges in the spaces after the roll. I did a little at Peter Bug but did not get to ride, not fully, across the chrome and black bridge. Practicing with Mickey, I showed him the roll as well as a version of it that began with smaller accented strokes on each rototom before opening up, full stick wings, above each drum. Most rototom players simply single stroke all the way across. That day at Mickey's, I showed him my emphasized roll, each stick digging into and out of the black dot, rapid intervals widening four times across four toms. It was a good workout. I felt confident afterwards. I had a plan. I was studying at American University. If I got into RE, I'd finish school in D.C. If I did not get in, I'd probably leave again. I was living at the upper mouth of Mount Pleasant in a very nice basement apartment that looked like an art gallery and I was working at AC MRDD (the Accreditation Council for Mentally Retarded and Other Developmentally Disabled Persons) as a compliance tabulator in Tenleytown, Wisconsin Avenue and Albemarle Street, N.W. The council was in the process of relocating to Boston and extending me an apartment in Back Bay for the summer if I wanted to join them. A huge part of me wanted to stay but the other huge part of me, the part that had lost some of the passion for staying up late in clubs and standing behind rototoms and timbales then sleeping late the next day, either wanted to leave or had already left. Leaving Mickey's, I was still undecided so I told myself I'd let the audition decide.

A few nights before the audition, I was visited by a few members of the band who called, unexpectedly, and asked if they could stop by. I should have been studying but I said yes. They bought me a gift, something of a test as I now see it. A message was sent; and were I to pass the audition, I would be accepting a different level of commitment than I had known in any other local band I had played with, a sort of brotherhood. This one came with perks, beautiful, ego-stroking luxuries. In 1980, I was 17 years old and was offered cocaine before my very first show. I declined. However, at 23, on the verge of, perhaps, joining the most popular band in the city, this somehow felt different. This was a rite of passage and while perhaps not a part of the actual audition, it did feel like a necessary part of a wider ritual. It was a great gift. It felt great. I thanked them and when they left, the gift left with them.

I was nervous all day. It rained all day. The rain was foreboding. Being a student of literature, the dark and wet day seemed to cast more omen than opportunity. I barely ate I was so nervous, so I took the S2 to P Street then transferred to the G2 back to the old neighborhood to get a haircut at Shabazz Barbershop, sat in Blinky's chair, was too nervous to argue with him. We always argued. It was Theater. And respect. I did not have a car. Floyd and DP picked me up before the sun went down. In the car, on the way to 851 Xenia Street, S.E., my body got hot and I got nauseous and then everything in the city, every nonhuman thing, waved at me as we passed it. I felt every bump of pavement and the bridge lasted forever. When we arrived, on the way up the steps Donnell turned to me and said, "Ok, once we get inside you don't have any friends." I already knew this but I was too busy trying to shake the nausea that had taken my legs. I was finally in the basement(s) of the two houses that made one practice spot, the birthplace of Rare Essence. I heard RE for the first time in 1978 and eight years later, I was in the basement with an opportunity to be a part of the next phase of the Total Groove. Roll Call: me, Mickey, Floyd, Footz, DP, Whiteboy and Ned. James Funk was there and not there at the same time, up and down the stairs a few times. Miss Mack watched for a few minutes and I think I saw Brady. Cabalou, surprisingly, did not come to the audition. I was sick to my stomach and lightheaded. Footz said let's start with "Display." I played it ok but not as well as I knew I could. I did not add anything to it, just played the pattern of it like the percussive math equation that it was, my favorite parts being the climb back to the smaller rototom to reset the sequence. "Display" was like the metronome of GoGo. It was a great way to tell if a percussionist could keep time without breaking time, falling out of time, or throwing the band off. I think I fell out of time once, maybe twice, during the audition but I also thought that I recovered well. After "Display," Footz said "Yeah, people think that the stuff that David plays is easy but it's not. He just makes it look easy." "The One On One," Whiteboy said. Footz hit the now-famous roll and we all went in, straight to the percussion, Footz and Mickey providing the foundation for me to click the rims and bounce between the two lower toms. We had been playing it for maybe a little more than a minute when Whiteboy stopped playing and said to me, "You ain't playing it right." "Yes, I am," I said. "No, you are not, how you gonna tell me," he said. "Because I have been watching this and playing this for years, you wrong man," I said, "Nah, that's it. I'm done, audition over," he said, and unplugged his guitar from the amp. Donnell said something like, "Sayers, don't worry about it," to prevent the argument from going any further. The light in the room became hospital harsh, whiter than the faces of the timbales. In ancient Greek, Xenia means hospitality and Zeus is often referred to as Zeus Xenios, the protector of strangers. Donnell and Derek Paige drove me back to Northwest. I was sick for two days but the rain made it easy to dry off in bed. The climate outside of the basement was still guarding me.

Quentin "Shorty Dud" Ivey and Milton "Go-Go Mickey" Freeman, 2009

Ricardo / Rickey "Sugar Foot" Wellman, 2012

Ricky Lyric Ky Ly Rick Ky Kick Key

Ricardo Dalvert Wellman
1955–2013

"Suga Foot, I gave him that name when he was a baby."
Chuck Brown

Mos' listnahs
outside-a Dee Cee
don't unnerstan', jes' don't
an' cain't keep up,
but lemme tell all y'all
'bout da las' foot
dat kick Chuck butt.
See now lemme teach it to ya
like ya in skool.
Ricky / Lyric Ky
Ly Rick Ky / Kick Key.
Mane wuz fast, fas' wo' a sweatband,
lak an athlete,
sho nuff tough,
nuthin' lak other drummas,
talk da talk mid hit,
could change yo hearing,
snare trap,
wit dat kick,
rhythm lak a reason
    to be intentional,
        hands deliberate,
            feet physical,
wha' dey call mono stereo steroids,
syllabic limb-feeling,

wha' dey call
a Metronomic Beat Reset,
da rudiments of da voltage of revolt,
da Revolution in da riot in a roll.
Blood sugar.
Blood count.
Blood pressure.
Ricky / Lyric Ky.
Bare-chested
and tom tom quantum,
a star rockin' stripes,
striped tube socks.
Word-play tuned to bottom.
None of dem udda drumma ass rumors
grow a home as long
'fo it wuz grown,
not lak Ricky.
He da first one
groom dat groove,
da las' one beat dat swing.
Da one, before all dem damn bullets,
made *hot chop barbeque*
so local known.
He Go.   He continuous.   He Go.
    Near a pio
  cursive person
    near a.
Ricky / Lyric Ky
Ly Rick Ky / Kick Key.
Him hymn him
our last Author Ricky,
soul searchin' fo' speech-fit,
heart da chest-seat center of-a foot-shaped spirit,

pocket-verb grievances,
a sacred architectural text,
breaking into
'sonic temples,
grammatical as anatomy,
anatomical as a clock's hand-busy
Remo face,
backseat lieutenant,
thunderous tempo a tenant
of un-equal
chrome housing,
numerology toe-numb,
Ricky / Lyric Ky / Kick Key,
one stick fo' addiction,
da udda fo' tour money,
love dem triple sweet triples,
one of dem Suga's,
lak a raw granulated inheritance,
substance a fuse,
must-a been his Daddy's.
   Gimme da bridge.
   Substructure Frank.
   Superstructure Ricky.
   Infrastructure Searcher.
Somebody lost the keys
but it fo' sho whatn' one-a dem.
Hah man, hah man.
Dhose days radio waves made us sick,
Ricky made us
well, man. Ricky,
like KK, years later,
so sickwitit. Ricky
made us well, man.

Mayor Marion Barry, 2012

The End of Our Village

One of those days when the sunlight and the light behind it, the daylight, were rubbing against each other in the sky like an atmospheric slow song between two different gears of crank creating the kind of heat, a soul-less humidity, that was white.

I would have preferred the yellow light of African or Brazilian cinema but the glass between us and the heavens, or crystalline canopy or whatever they were calling it this epoch, was more in the mood of a magnifying glass.

One of those days when the buildings sweated glare, neither wet or dry, just bright, miracle-blinding, homegoing light.

One of those blinding days, when even the parts of the shade known for disciplining August, was light-skinned.

One of those days I decided to walk, camera-walk, from near the D.C. Wharf in Southwest (through federal downtown) to the bottom of Shaw.

A funeral day, that kind of day. A day named and given a date by an Emperor, Constantine, the adjuster of the Julian Calendar to its current Gregorian form. This is how they mark it. This is how they write it. This is how they say it: May 31, 2012.

A day carrying bibles beyond the goodbyes. A day God gets a piece of its body back. A day when the parts of a huge departure are broken into the spare parts of many smaller departures.

Because I once knew the city intimately, I could see through the mascara of unfinished plans even as their instruments of construction made a music capable of placing tombstones with windows in them around our neighborhoods. I could smell the embalming fluid of money turning itself into a trendy street drug often enough to make their businesses and buildings last.

Crossing the intersection of 7th and Massachusetts and New York Avenues, I was in a sun daze, wiping sweat from my eyelids as the people, who looked like ants, came into focus and got slightly larger, and I do mean slightly.

The lines were long and the mood of the people waiting to be admitted into the Washington Convention Center was the same as if they were waiting for the Godfather of GoGo to perform. Looking North, I could see The Gibson Plaza Apartments where I lived as a kid until High School Graduation and where Roderick Smith whom we called Top Flight Raj first turned me onto the Soul Searchers and boosting, but everything else was, mostly, gone, eliminated when the city inserted a Metro System of tunnels and trains into the ground.

Gone were the elders who used to sit in windows and watch us challenge each other as we busted-up summer. Gone were the empty lots of car bodies that looked like their metal and rubber organs had been harvested.

I arrived early. The concrete was lit, not enlightened, just lit, giving back to the sun what the sun had partially taught it, enough heat left behind to suggest a clear haze of water that made the day look like it was already a memory. Once conductive, the urban crust is now always covered. People wore various t-shirts that paid homage to Chuck, mostly to the period of his rebranding as a mafioso figure.

Sharp Suit. Hat. Shades. Cigar.

The silky rainforest of his Jheri Curl Period did not make it onto any of the memorial t-shirts. Muscular Chuck was dead but Pops was alive and built deeply into the city by the city to be used by the city. A homegrown import from North Carolina. A son of Gaston.

One of those days when everyone wanted to be photographed, a chance to become officially a part of, at least visually, the historical record. Stacks of newspapers, *The Washington Post*, featuring Chuck as a figure on a tarot card, were placed like sandbags and bundles at the corners of the block.

Gone were the men who stood on corners just talking to each other, men who leaned against cars and creased their pants with knives of heat. There was a difference between slacks and double knits but the ability to know that difference was gone too.

I worked the lines, all film, several times before going inside. I felt immediately trusted. I ran into an old crush, Michelle. She was with Peanut, her best friend from childhood who I hadn't seen since the 1980s. Peanut's Chuck outfit was on-point. I also ran into my old running-buddy Nico "the GoGo-Ologist" Hobson, the founder and director of GoGoRadio, and vocalist Ms. Kim. I photographed them together. I peeped "BJ," GoGo Mickey's son, in line near the main public entrance, and snapped him. In the photograph, he looks like he's underwater, a youngin' with a 'frohawk swimming in non-blur, an invisible hyphen of heat like the one I snatched from the word GoGo (throughout these notes) between us.

Inside, I made an interesting color portrait of Peanut while she sat in a chair in an open space. The image has Neo Soul written all over it and no traces of the solemn energy of a funeral. Of all of the portraits I took that day, a black and white medium shot of Halima Peru holding the funeral program with Chuck's face on it, strikes a chord of loss "each and every time I see it" as Chuck would say. Folks had come, truly, to celebrate his life not mourn a loss. Their city that had been changing, had finally changed for good.

Gone were the stores and shops that looked like they were owned by people they knew. Gone was the constant street chatter of a familiar accent and slang.

All of the seats in the main hall were empty. Programs had been placed in the seats, the first several rows (center and adjacent) all reserved for family and local dignitaries. From a large screen above the stage, Chuck's face looked over the entire hall. It was cool Chuck, mid-life Chuck, part down-home country boy, part money-making hustler.

For the next two hours, I did not sit down or stop moving. I roamed the audience, backstage, the sign-in tables, conversations between family members, the moods of the speakers, politicians and wanna-be politicians. Ayre Rayde sat with Ayre Rayde. Junk sat with Junk. Be'la Dona and Suttle were scattered. Shannon Browne, Be'la Dona's drummer, cried as hard as anyone in the funeral. Pretti Nikki mourned as if in a song, her face a soft, brown, treble clef of loss. Adrienne "DreDre" Burkley (from Horu Experience) and JuJu sat together. There wasn't any life in JuJu's face. He looked hurt, hurt again, and like the timing of this new hurt would add a longer lasting hurt to all of the other hurts.

Near the end of the service, Chuck's last band, the Chuck Brown Band (not the Soul Searchers) performed. They were joined by various members of the GoGo Community: Sugar Bear, James Funk, Big Tony and Whiteboy. It was the most crowded stage I'd ever seen at a GoGo-related event. Family members, musicians, radio personalities, comedians.

DJ Kool was funnier than Mike Epps, "I am a graduate from GoGo University. I graduated at the top of my class, Darn it. Magna cum laude. Chuck Brown was my Professor. I got a Master's Degree in the art of Call and Response. I'm a proud graduate of GoGo University. DMV, I represent all day, every day. Chuck Brown, we love you madly. We love you madly. GoGo cum laude!" I had never heard laude sound like Lordy but I could not laugh.

Chuck Brown was dead and our village, the former District of Coloreds, was ending again. All of the little churches that were squeezed between little houses were gone, not a hand-painted sign yelled anything of significance, not too many nice non-chain food joints around for miles.

I photographed Marion Barry, sitting up front, reading the program. He looked extremely comfortable—like he had lots of leg room, like he was riding a clean Metro Bus, let's say the 30 bus, from Southeast, through downtown, through Georgetown, up Wisconsin Avenue (past the National Cathedral where Benny and Melita were married) to Chevy Chase. While Chuck lay in a casket and Vincent Gray and Eleanor Norton Holmes were on stage, Barry sat with the folk like he sitting at the back of a bus in a gray suit studying for an exam. I spoke to him, "Hello Mayor Barry."

We'd done this before. Him in my lens. Flash.

He barely moved. The light between us dissolved and I walked away, to the next picture, through the door the brief light made.

After changing my rolls of film so many times, I got that feeling I used to get onstage, the feeling of what next and wow, we've only played three songs but (to my body), it feels like five, that feeling of experiencing two different moments of time at once, one physical and the other mental, swimming and walking, so next (being no next at all just the feeling of in between), I did what you would have done if you were standing at a funeral and the body had just been loaded into the hearse and the crowd was watching it drive-by on the way out of the side door of the massive Convention Center.

I did what you would have done if you had three cameras strapped to you, two Leicas and a Nikon, and all of sudden Tom Goldfogle, Chuck's last manager, pointed toward the large opening where the sun was reaching in to meet the hearse while you had been trying to photograph the facial expressions of the drivers.

White, coachmen-like and very focused in their lonely offices of Otherness, driver and passenger. No language left them, no emotion I could name. Swedish, German? Their vibe was that of a wind that was uninterested in its own ability to blow but one that was uniformed in the service of helping souls to cross. Their hired numbness was unlike any of the other numbnesses. Maybe they didn't expect the party. Hard to be professional while the natives are raising the dead, while, trusted to their care was a cultural worker of the higher order, a builder, one that could not be defined by the symbolic form of an ornament of modernity or a hood ornament.

The Spirit of Ecstasy. When will my eyes see? It was the Godfather of GoGo not just anyone. A Rolls-Royce not just any vehicle for hearing salvation, not just any hearsay of leaving or hearse. A Rolls. One of the voices of royalty headed home. Driven. Called. A roll. A call. A remixture.

A voice is a vehicle. The British line of Charles. The French line of Louis. The Native Line of Brown. What would you have done if you turned toward the hearse and there was Darryl Brooks, again, by his side, again, to the very end as if protecting him? Would you have taken the picture?

Gone were the records stores as well as the blind man who sang on the corner of 9th and F, gone. Lancaster, who refereed so many playground recreational center and Boy's Club games, gone. Barbara Sizemore, gone.

Step closer to the window, lean inward, the lean limited by respect.

Casket top and flowers through glass, the sun behind everything: background becoming foreground, foreground becoming background, each leaving an element of its composition in the frame for the other to decompose—like a medley of reflections with recognizable origins but unrecognizable destinies. The image of me shooting into the hearse window was made by the sun not scissors. It is a single exposure, a fo(lk)cal frame and fusion of me and Chuck. An in-the-camera creation assisted by Kodak Portra 160 Color Film.

The outline of me in a shutter ghost of Chuck. The sun behind the sun. The sun behind a father. The sun behind a son. The Pops of all sons. Light entering the flowers on the casket. The flowers curling, tighter, like soft hearts, in response. I had to decide where to focus, the lines of the casket, the blooms, or my own reflection. Someone, not sure who, was watching. It must have looked odd. I rushed myself. Outdoors in the sun, all alone with Chuck Brown's hearse, I didn't know what to do.

In my head, in the chamber of the camera: the visual voice of the source again. Spirit, a creation reversal, "pir" instead of "RIP." Camera alchemy, alchemical literacy. The flowers on me, a flow, ritualized me, the whole frame coming together in the service of physical rest—no longer a rectangle but still a frame.

Chuck Brown Way, an offering. Again. The living city was offering him a way out, a way to become one of its eternal signs and symbols, alive, one of its living crossroads. The day the street was dedicated to him as a Way, it rained—in the body of the city and from his face. I photographed him crying. He held the sign and seemed to embrace the sign. In his name, the Way embraced him. The way was everywhere, all over T Street and the folks who loved him behaved a certain way that day. To help alter the identity of the street, they danced till they were wet. Umbrellas like the flowers to come, facing up, like the shiny sex organs of a garden. All colors, including red tops. He wore a cross. Another game, another seven. The game of 7th and T, the Tau cross, was almost over. From the stage, he saw the place where they would view the first stage of his rest. A tearful irony becoming drench.

Here's the thing, the party roll, that no one will want to hear: Certain hairstyles (especially the Jheri Curl) helped some Black People hide their pre-Native Americanness and helped others embrace it. In the case of Chuck Louis Brown, his was enhanced. Seeing him through a lens so many times, this is what I noticed. He was not African American not in the Government definition of African American. He was Pre-Native

American. His people were already here before America was America. He was more than American. He was extra but with style. That was his bamma, his other side.

Another other side imprisoned in an inferior vessel. GoGo is from here not from the other side of the Atlantic, here. If y'all keep calling his name, if y'all keep remembering him and naming things after him, he will (either) never leave or he will come back sooner. Let him go. There are many things, now, other than sacred angles and angels to be one with.

The Real H Street, gone. Grooving gone. Neighborhood rivalries and corner stores with ice machines outside, gone. Real ass parades gone. Petey Greene gone. They tore down the second version of Dunbar and built a third one. John Gaverick's Advanced Grammar and Composition Class gone. My view of my own shoes, gone. Olshausen, gone. Morton's, McBride's and Cavalier's all gone.

Mayor4Life soon to be gone again and gone. The Spook who sat by the door and did what the door told him to do, Frank Wills, gone. Buckets gone.

If GoGo means to keep going, what is gone? To be still or still be here, him through me, me through him, no matter the mode, medium or form. The last picture I took of him made us one. We are the author of an author's photo.

One of those days it was hard to tell what direction the sunlight was coming from, sky or ground, ride or crash? One of those days heat and hurt made the cameras heavier, so I imagined a time when the entire Earth was as light as a feather and not yet a pool liquid of photographic developer full of images that had yet to become souls, all swimming between the front and rear elements of lens glass.

Left up to me, eye-weary me, not another photograph would be born, taken or given, anywhere else in the world, that kind of day, no photographs in available light, no flash, until the village rid itself of the shooters and the mutes and not until it resisted, with a percussive integrity, being forced into little blocks on a grid of garden-less, concrete elegies. One of those days.

The wonderful things of the Golden Age, gone.

Bootleg Chuck Tees for Sale, 2012

III

The pocket in question is a small pocket of resistance.

John Berger

Steps Toward a GoGo Revolution

On February 19, 2020, Mayor Muriel Bowser signed the GoGo Music of the District of Columbia Designation Act of 2019 to make GoGo the Official Music of Washington, D.C.

[1]

Because nothing is more easily fooled than the ear, we have to evict the influence of radio and excessive covers from Go-Go not Go-Go Radio or GoGo from the Radio. The constant memorization of songs containing the values of other individuals constricts creative growth. If you listen very closely, over time, you will hear that the values expressed in the heavily rotated songs are the same values hidden in the products being advertised between those songs and on radio talk shows. These values, expressed mostly as drinking and ass-talk have found their way into GoGo, dominating the creative focus of youth and adult output. A minimum ten-year withdrawal to thoroughly flush the long-term programming, keeping in mind that radio waves were once considered a form of pandemic-inducing poison. After Go-Go is healthy and original again, then those who still feel obedient to radio can ease back into aspects of it with a renewed and healthier sense of self defense and taste for what is worthy of their efforts. Disguised as a friend and soulful nutrient, the cultural skin of corporate radio is actually an enemy of the people.

[2]

In the same way that marching band, the ritual militarization of music, is offered, every local public high school should house an active GoGo Band, Ensemble or Orchestra, so that the act of learning the rules of English and the various levels of Math healthily mix and mingle with the act of learning the rules of the pocket, the various grammars, gears, and sockets active within Crank and Bounce. Imagine "The One On One" taught as a multiple, compound-complex run-on groove or "The Roll

Call," any roll call of names, as a strict sonnet sequence of organized couplets, a Shakespearian "Shake It, (But Don't Break It)." Consider "E-Flat Boogie" as geometric theorem, "Shake It Like A White Girl" as the inverse of Ethnic Studies. At the core of Crank is curriculum and the circumference of cultural circle is a commitment to the percussive coursework of community, a coup d'etat tat tat tat ta boom.

[3]

Storm the Monuments, the Museums, the Smithsonian basements, the tunnels under the National Mall. Own downtown. Stop being stage-hidden. Live everywhere, every ward, park, café and quadrant. Be a presence on the city's art scene. Be present in the social spaces of the People, black and white, who come to your home for school and jobs. Super grit on them so hard it "knocks da socks off-da foots." Make them uncomfortable in their intentions, their protected intentions. Make them take the energy (you put on them) home with them. Furthermore: anyone caught smuggling tapes, CDs, videos or photographs outside of the beltway, will have both of their hands cut off and placed in the crowded barrels of crabs under Rasheeda Moore's bribed eyes. Time to close the door and fix shit, Da One purpose. The first Charter of our anti-Congress will be shaped like and sound like two old tambourines, wooden and interlocked, a percussive pleasure proclamation, two rings no rod, the sting of stinginess and the sovereign socket, reinstated.

[4]

No more band member sharing, except for cases of extreme emergency or as a Special Guest, sometimes, not until the sound is repaired. Choose a band, play with that band. Grow and gel with that set of musicians so that a distinct community sound will emerge. Crank sameness, like a parasite from the inside-out, is thinning the originality and vitality of GoGo. A distinct sound is the key to longevity and success even if it takes a while to catch on locally. A distinct sound is not necessarily created by having the best musicians. More often, in GoGo, it is achieved by musicians who have grown together and who are unafraid to make mistakes and explore each other. No more dress alike or sound alike crank. Crank is not a costume. A return to analog mixing might also help.

[5]

The Crank Age of Onstage Sound Design is ready to go physical and ready to go live so let's vary the architectural positioning of the structures onstage according to band sound not traditional band set-up. The conga player up front and center. Drummer on a platform behind the conga player. Lead Talker behind the drummer on an even higher platform. No reason for the horns, stuck in horn lines, to stand together. No reason for the guitarist to ever be limited by cords. Keyboards next to the sound board, command control. Spread the vocalist, lead talker included, throughout the audience. Give the cowbell, tambourine, vibra-slap, blocks and rototoms to the bartenders, security, and the regulars to play during the show! In the future, the physical will come last. Pay the promoter to make the stage look like an art ruin.

[6]

It may be time to dismantle The Total Groove/Wickedest Band Alive Industrial Complex so that its legacy can properly reset and refuel the GoGo scene by distributing all of its active, former and current members into the contemporary gene pool of crank. Like a talisman or a sigil, so many of the classic older live recordings have reached the status of Community Power Objects and their magic cannot be surpassed. This is the secret of the Highland tape; it is not simply a recording; it is a brew and there will be no true youth Revolution as long as the disembodied echoes of it are active among us. To continue to compete with such a memory of the self within the current scene may prove to be counter-damage-groove-productive in the long run. Once you have reached the height numerous times, the height becomes a floor.

[7]

Only a complete re-embracing of both timelines of the JYB Purpose can fully extend the JYB Possibility. There is nothing more potent and dynamic than a full Junk Yard Band Family socket and nothing more visually representative of the coming victory of D.C. folklife over Washington Bureaucracy than the integrated sight of the classic Junk Yard buckets and cans mixed with so-called real musical instruments. By juxtaposing indestructible plastic and the hardware technology and chrome, Junk can provide an example of hybrid city-mending, while introducing a socket so syncretic it resurrects the best properties of the Silver Age of GoGo. When BU winks, Winko creeps through the hoodoo of vanishing hoods. Their Art House, the sound surrealism of Avant-Farm Crank, is the biggest house.

[8]

In the late 70s and 80s, GoGo hurt itself by building a social wall around itself and not allowing tape recorders and cameras into the shows. As a result, GoGo has no substantial record of its Golden Age, Bucket Age and most of the Silver Age. The lack of images and recordings from this period is lazily-criminal. GoGo's attitude toward local, non-GoGo artists must change. The doors must open and stay open and GoGo must find a way to embrace and collaborate with (not merely use) poets, photographers, painters, writers, journalists and musicians from other genres, etc. without being paranoid, rude, cheap or losing its center. GoGo has grown slow, too damn slow, thus, an all-around art sense is one of the necessary pieces to the upper-middle stage of its survival.

[9]

GoGo must now feed the mind and turn to the rich tradition of Black and indigenous, global musical history—history not being a past but a possibility that moves away from the past into the unknown, the explorative, the experimental. And while the fabric of the pocket might be sewn or locked too tightly to allow its contents to percussively come and go as they please, it is still a worthy foundation capable of holding and upholding anything placed within it or on top of it: Marley, Fela, Ellington, Simone, Masekela. Weensey soaring through "Mississippi Goddamn." Adia Doores, Halima Peru, Tylisa Brown, Kimise Lee and God-bold Pammy Pam Ward putting their foot in a Dope Jam version of "Sorrow, Tears and Blood." Steve Roy mixing Lenny Williams with the experimental explorations of Jeanne Lee. Michael Muse, Kal-El Gross and LaKindra Shane'a breezing through Sun Ra's "Space is the Place," adlibs by Brian "Whop" Craig and Lavert "T-Bob" Cole. I already know Bootsy Vegas would slice-sice "If I Woz A Tap-Notch Poet" by Linton Kwesi Johnson. I am not advocating for better cover songs. I am challenging GoGo to alter the formula and the compositional structure of many of its now predictable approaches to Crank. A new crank-shaped crank, a revitalized percussive alphabet, the bones of the lexicon, is local-global not local-national and must resist the movement of a mathematical equation.

[10]

Despite the Designation Act of 2019 to make GoGo the Official Music of D.C., GoGo should cease all social and business transactions with the local and federal government. If it wants to be, truly be, considered an independent art form, it must separate its purpose and mission from reliance on the city. It must adopt the attitude that the city grew from GoGo not that GoGo grew from the city. Reliance becomes servitude quicker than pushing and shoving can ruin a show. GoGo should also exercise more discretion when working with very popular Hip Hop personalities because many of them arrive in the District of Crank with a well-planned and well-assigned agenda in hand. Crank is surrounded by many Neo False Face Societies, all of whom must be unmasked, immediately. GoGo needs a government detox. "Go head, go head, go head" means heads must roll. The chant is also meant to suggest a transference of power, the coming of an inevitable Folk Dynasty. A rejection of the forces capable of raising any one individual above the rest of the community because being raised above the city like a star or shepherd (to be followed) is, over time, a more violent act than shooting up the neighborhood.

Note on the Author

Thomas Sayers Ellis was born and raised in Washington, D.C. where he attended Paul Laurence Dunbar High School. In 1988, he co-founded The Dark Room Collective in Cambridge, Massachusetts. He worked at the Grolier Poetry Bookshop in Harvard Square and studied with Seamus Heaney and Lucie Brock-Broido before attending Brown University where he earned an MFA in Creative Writing under the tutelage of Michael S. Harper. He is the author of *The Maverick Room, Skin, Inc.: Identity Repair Poems* and *The Corny Toys*, a chapbook-length poem. His writing has appeared in Best American Poetry (1997, 2001, 2010, 2015), *The Paris Review, Straight No Chaser, Tin House, Poetry, The Nation* and numerous anthologies. Ellis has taught at Case Western University, Sarah Lawrence College, the University of San Francisco, Wesleyan University, the University of Montana, Bennington College and Lesley University Low-Residency MFA Programs and the Iowa Writers Workshop. He is the recipient of a Mrs. Giles Whiting Writers Award and was awarded a Guggenheim Fellowship for Poetry in 2015.

His photography has appeared in *Art & Letters, CutBank, Poetry, Columbia, Goldenseal, Jubilat, Lumina, Vox Populi, Prairie Schooner, Reverie, Taint Taint Taint, Tuesday, An Art Project, Transition, Pluck!* and *Indiana Review* as well as in numerous documentaries, and on CDs and book covers.

He presented the first exhibition of GoGo Photography, "(Un) Lock It: The Percussive People in the GoGo Pocket" in 2011 at the Gallery at Vivid Solutions in Washington, D.C. In 2013, he exhibited "The Offense of Regular Black Self Defense" in Round 38 at Project Row Houses in Houston, Texas. At the same time, he was featured in "D.C. As I See It," a juried exhibition at the Leica Gallery Store in Washington, D.C., and in 2019, "Manually Forcing All Modes of ReSKINstance Into Fo(lk)cus," a solo exhibition of photographs, was presented at Studio 81 in Mantova, Italy.

In 2014, he co-founded (with saxophonist James Brandon Lewis), Heroes Are Gang Leaders, a literary jazz ensemble of writers and musicians. In 2018, after four CD releases, HAGL was awarded the American Book Award for Oral Literature. In 2019, the ensemble was signed to Ropeadope Records, releasing its most ambitious project to date, *Artificial Happiness Button*. HAGL has performed in Paris, Bordeaux, Berlin, The Hague, Gdansk, Lisbon, New York City and Washington, D.C.

Reflection of TSE Shooting Chuck Brown's Casket through Hearse Window, 2012

A<small>RROWSMITH</small> is named after the late William Arrowsmith, a renowned classics scholar, literary and film critic. General editor of thirty-three volumes of *The Greek Tragedy in New Translations*, he was also a brilliant translator of Eugenio Montale, Cesare Pavese, and others. Arrowsmith, who taught for years in Boston University's University Professors Program, championed not only the classics and the finest in contemporary literature, he was also passionate about the importance of recognizing the translator's role in bringing the original work to life in a new language.

Like the arrowsmith who turns his arrows straight and true,
a wise person makes his character straight and true.

— Buddha

Books by
ARROWSMITH PRESS

Girls by Oksana Zabuzhko
Bula Matari/Smasher of Rocks by Tom Sleigh
This Carrying Life by Maureen McLane
Cries of Animal Dying by Lawrence Ferlinghetti
Animals in Wartime by Matiop Wal
Divided Mind by George Scialabba
The Jinn by Amira El-Zein
Bergstein edited by Askold Melnyczuk
Arrow Breaking Apart by Jason Shinder
Beyond Alchemy by Daniel Berrigan
*Conscience, Consequence: Reflections on
Father Daniel Berrigan* edited by Askold Melnyczuk
Ric's Progress by Donald Hall
Return To The Sea by Etnairis Rivera
The Kingdom of His Will by Catherine Parnell
Eight Notes from the Blue Angel by Marjana Savka
Fifty-Two by Melissa Green
Music In—And On—The Air by Lloyd Schwartz
Magpiety by Melissa Green
Reality Hunger by William Pierce
Soundings: On The Poetry of Melissa Green edited by Sumita Chakraborty
The Corny Toys by Thomas Sayers Ellis
Black Ops by Martin Edmunds
Museum of Silence by Romeo Oriogun
City of Water by Mitch Manning
Passeggiate by Judith Baumel
Persephone Blues by Oksana Lutsyshyna
The Uncollected Delmore Schwartz edited by Ben Mazer
The Light Outside by George Kovach
The Blood of San Gennaro by Scott Harney edited by Megan Marshall
No Sign by Peter Balakian
Firebird by Kythe Heller
The Selected Poems of Oksana Zabuzhko edited by Askold Melnyczuk
The Age of Waiting by Douglas J. Penick
Manimal Woe by Fanny Howe